Street by St

WATFORD

BOREHAMWOOD, BUSHEY, RICKMANSWORTH

Abbots Langley, Bricket Wood, Carpenders Park, Chorleywood, Croxley Green, Elstree, Kings Langley, Oxhey, Radlett

2nd edition April 2008
© Automobile Association Developments Limited 2008

Original edition printed September 2002

This product includes map data licensed from Ordnance Survey® with the permission of the Controller of Her Majesty's Stationery Office. © Crown copyright 2008. All rights reserved. Licence number 100021153.

Published by AA Publishing (a trading name of Automobile Association Developments Limited, whose registered office is Fanum House, Basing View, Basingstoke, Hampshire RG21 4EA. Registered number 1878835).

Produced by the Mapping Services Department of The Automobile Association. (A03557)

A CIP Catalogue record for this book is available from the British Library.

Printed by Oriental Press in Dubai

Ref: ML188z

Key to map pages	ii-iii
Key to map symbols	iv-1
Enlarged map pages	2-3
Main map pages	4-35
Index – towns & villages	36
Index – streets	37-43
Index – featured places	43-44
Acknowledgements	44

ii

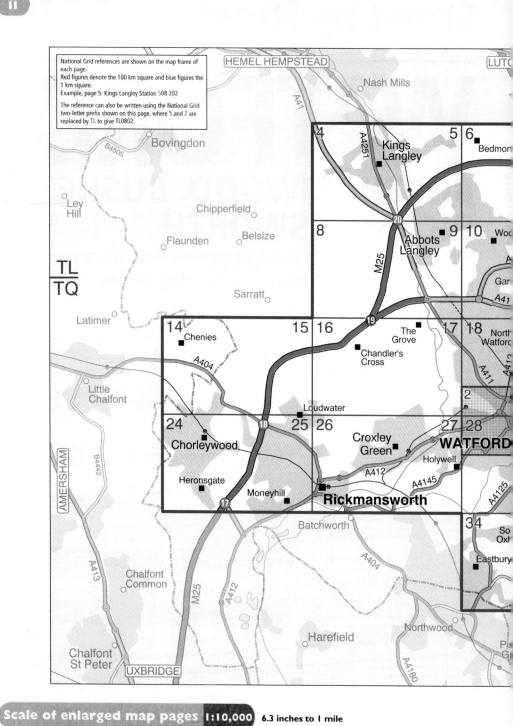

National Grid references are shown on the map frame of each page.
Red figures denote the 100 km square and blue figures the 1 km square.
Example, page 5: Kings Langley Station 508 202

The reference can also be written using the National Grid two-letter prefix shown on this page, where 5 and 2 are replaced by TL to give TL0802.

HEMEL HEMPSTEAD   LUTO

Nash Mills

Bovingdon

Ley Hill

Chipperfield

Flaunden   Belsize

TL
TQ

Sarratt

Latimer

Chenies

Little Chalfont

14

A404

Kings Langley

4   5   6
                  Bedmon

8   9   10
Abbots   Wo
Langley

15 16   The Grove   17 18
                              North
Chandler's Cross   Watfor

Loudwater   2

24   25 26   Croxley   27 28
Chorleywood   Green   WATFORD
                                  Holywell
Heronsgate   A412
Moneyhill   A4145
Rickmansworth

Batchworth   34
                          So
                          Oxh
A404   Eastbury

Chalfont Common

AMERSHAM

M25 A412

Harefield

Northwood

Chalfont St Peter

UXBRIDGE

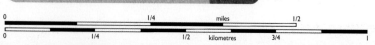

Scale of enlarged map pages 1:10,000   6.3 inches to 1 mile

0   1/4   miles   1/2
0   1/4   1/2   kilometres   3/4   1

MEL HEMPSTEAD

Chiswell
Green

M10

1

Park
Street

A1081

HERTFORD

A414

STEVENAGE

Welham
Green

How
Wood

A405

21a

cket
ood

A5183

B5378

London
Colney

A1081

2

M25

M25

A1(M)

Brookmans
Park

A1081

B556

B556

South
Mimms

| 11 | 12 | | 13 |

M1

Radlett

B462

Shenley

Ridge

South
Mimms

6

TL
TQ

A1081

| 19 | 20 | | 21 | 22 | | 23 |

5

Aldenham

Letchmore
Heath

A5183

Green
Street

B5378

Borehamwood

Well
End

A1

A411

| 29 | 30 | | 31 | 32 | | 33 |

B462

A41

A411

A411

Barnet

Arkley

A5109

B552

A411

Bushey

Bushey
Heath

Elstree

4

London
Gateway

| 35 |

A4008

penders
k

B4542

h End

A4140

A409

A410

Stanmore

A41

A4140

A409

Harrow
Weald

A404

A5

Edgware

M1

Highwood
Hill

Mill
Hill

A1

B552

A5109

2

HARROW

LONDON LONDON

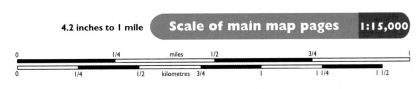

4.2 inches to 1 mile   **Scale of main map pages**   **1:15,000**

| 0 | | 1/4 | | miles | 1/2 | | 3/4 | | 1 |

| 0 | 1/4 | | 1/2 | kilometres | 3/4 | | 1 | | 1 1/4 | | 1 1/2 |

iv

Junction 9 — Motorway & junction	*LC* — Level crossing
Services — Motorway service area	Tramway
Primary road single/dual carriageway	Ferry route
Services — Primary road service area	Airport runway
A road single/dual carriageway	County, administrative boundary
B road single/dual carriageway	Mounds
Other road single/dual carriageway	**17** Page continuation 1:15,000
Minor/private road, access may be restricted	**3** Page continuation to enlarged scale 1:10,000
← One-way street	River/canal, lake, pier
Pedestrian area	Aqueduct, lock, weir
Track or footpath	465 ▲ Winter Hill — Peak (with height in metres)
Road under construction	Beach
Road tunnel	Woodland
P Parking	Park
P+ Park & Ride	Cemetery
Bus/coach station	Built-up area
Railway & main railway station	Industrial/business building
Railway & minor railway station	Leisure building
Underground station	Retail building
Light railway & station	Other building
Preserved private railway	

⊓⊓⊓⊓⊓⊓⊓	City wall		♜	Castle
A&E	Hospital with 24-hour A&E department		🏛	Historic house or building
PO	Post Office		Wakehurst Place (NT)	National Trust property
📖	Public library		Ⓜ	Museum or art gallery
i	Tourist Information Centre		♞	Roman antiquity
i	Seasonal Tourist Information Centre		⊥	Ancient site, battlefield or monument
🗋 🗋	Petrol station, 24 hour Major suppliers only		⊶	Industrial interest
†	Church/chapel		✤	Garden
🚻	Public toilets		◉	Garden Centre Garden Centre Association Member
♿	Toilet with disabled facilities		⚘	Garden Centre Wyevale Garden Centre
PH	Public house AA recommended		♠	Arboretum
⦿	Restaurant AA inspected		⛢	Farm or animal centre
Madeira Hotel ⌐	Hotel AA inspected		⚘	Zoological or wildlife collection
🎭	Theatre or performing arts centre		�	Bird collection
🎥	Cinema		⌐	Nature reserve
⚑	Golf course		◀◀	Aquarium
▲	Camping AA inspected		**V**	Visitor or heritage centre
⊡	Caravan site AA inspected		⍩	Country park
▲⊡	Camping & caravan site AA inspected		◔	Cave
⏃	Theme park		✹	Windmill
⛪	Abbey, cathedral or priory		⬡	Distillery, brewery or vineyard

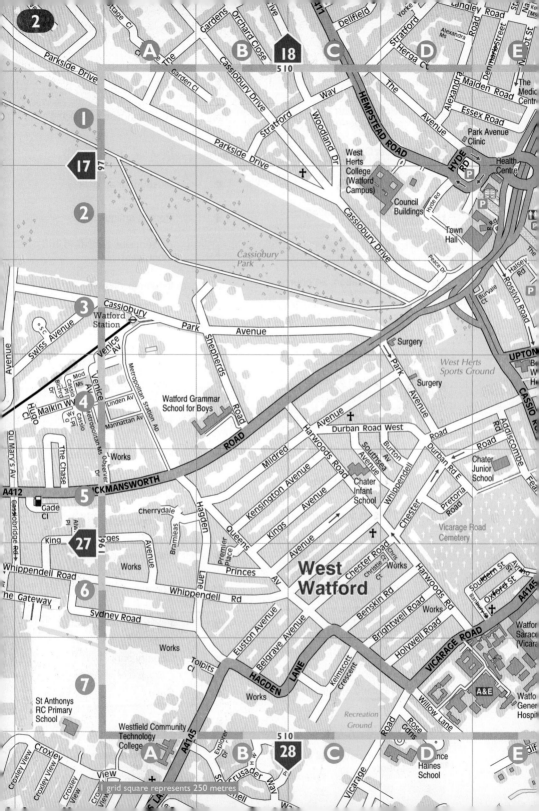

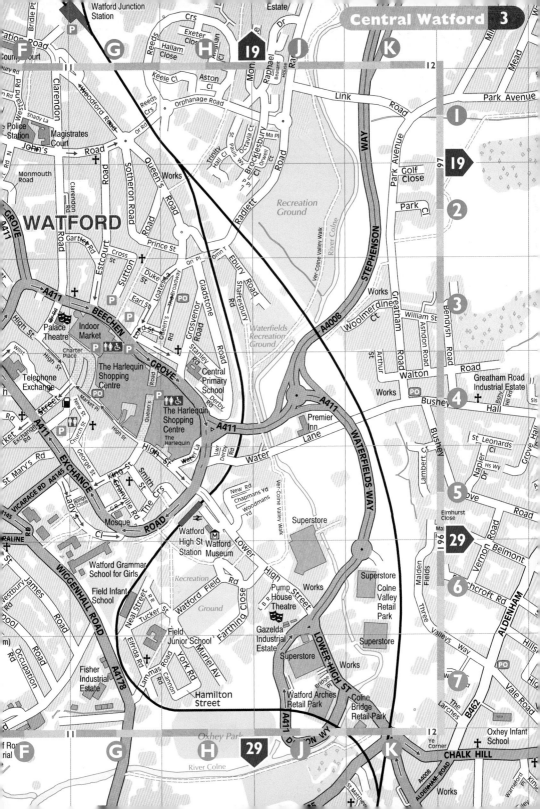

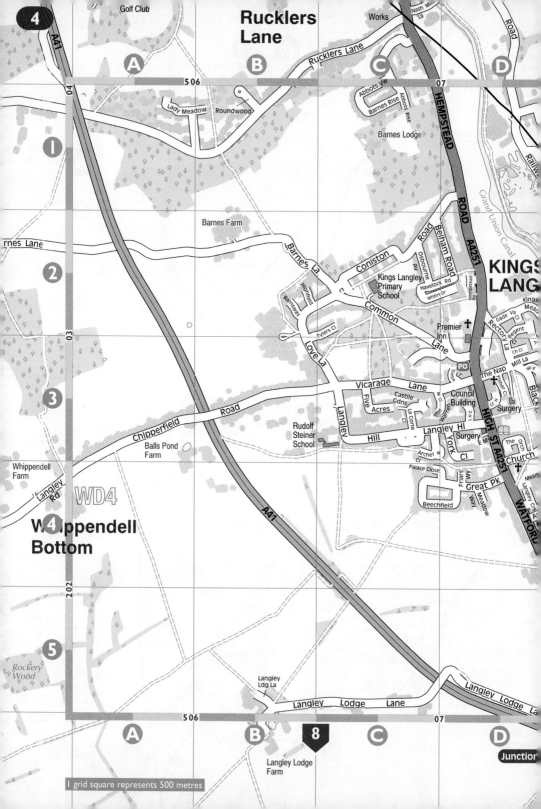

Hyde Farm

Hyde Lane

Hart Hall

Bedmond

E **F** **G** **H**

08 09 04

Hyde Lane

I

Bluebell Dr

Tom's Lane

Meadow Wy

Bedmond JMI School

Harthall Lane

Harthall Lane

Hilltop Rd

Seabrook Rd

Tom's Lane

Tom's Lane

Tom's Lane

2

Woodlands Dr

Shaftesbury Wy

Grosvenor Av

Belgrave Drive

Tom's La

Grosvenor Sq

Sheppey's La

Bedmond Road

03

alley

Hil

Kings Park Industrial Estate

unberland

Grand Union Canal Wlk

Numbers Farm

M25

3

6

Abbots Langley Primary School

Parsonage

Love La

Tibbs Hill Rd

Summerhou

Parnell

High St

Station Rd

La

Roman Gdns

Works

Egg Farm Lane

St Lawrence Cl

Breakspear

The Crs

4

TIDS Hill Rd

underland

st

Works

Kings Langley Station

Abbots Road

Abbots Road

Dellmeadow

Standfield

St

PO

High St

Langley Road

Creasy Cl

cil ng

Home Park Industrial Estate

e Park Mill Link Rd

Ltl Howe Cre

Abbots Road

Manor House Gdns

Surgery

Adrian Road

Marli Sq

Cherry Hollow

5

Rise

Folle

Kindersley

Way

Gallows Hill

Gallows Hill

Lane

Pope's Rd

Gallows

Breakspeare Road

Trowley

Wadham La Wy

Berkeley Cl

Queens Dr

Keble Ter

Shirley Cl

Edward Cl

E **F** **G** **H**

08 09

Gallows Hill

Gallows

Gallows

ne Saviour Prim School

Hill

Rise

Broomfield

Ac

Little Oren

Deans

Greenways

Breakspeare School

Oak Gn

Furtherfield Rd

Havitand Wy

De Frthrf

9

Hazelbur Av

Oak Tree Cl

Tanners Wood La

Tanners Wood Primary School

River Gade

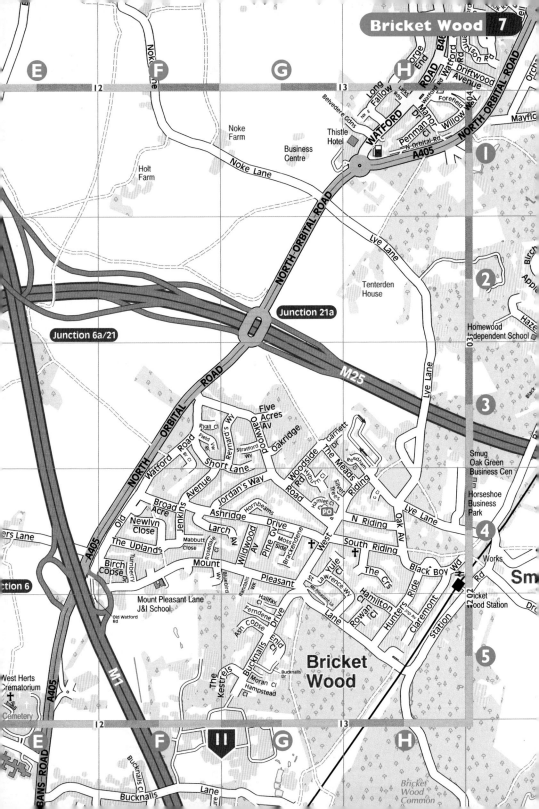

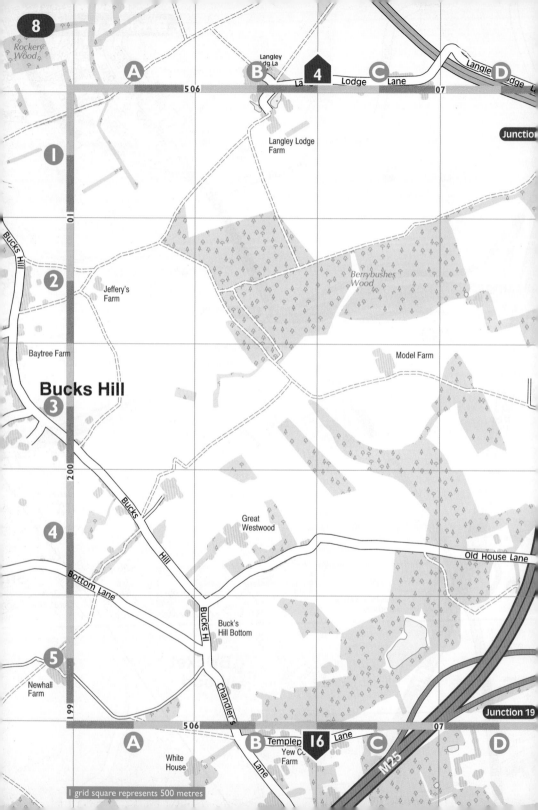

8

Rockery Wood

A 5 06 **B** Langley Ldg La **4** La Lodge Lane **C** 07 Langle Lodge La **D**

Junction

I

Bucks Hill

Langley Lodge Farm

2

Jeffery's Farm

Berrybushes Wood

Baytree Farm

Model Farm

Bucks Hill

3

Bucks Hill

4

Great Westwood

Old House Lane

Bottom Lane

Buck's Hill Bottom

5

Chandler's

Newhall Farm

Junction 19

A 5 06 **B** Temple **16** Lane **C** 07 **D**

White House

Yew C Farm

M25

I grid square represents 500 metres

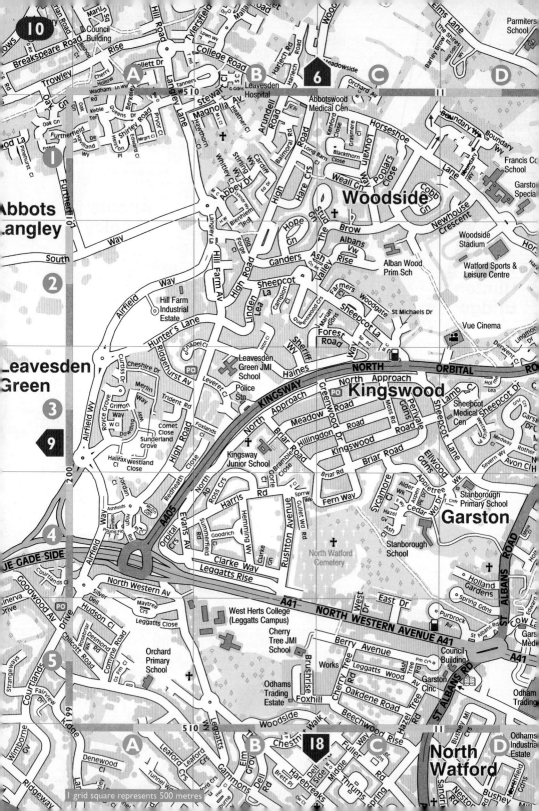

Bricket
Wood

West Herts
Crematorium

Cemetery

Bricket
Wood
Common

Little Mu
Farm

School Lane

Ver-Colne Valley Walk

Meriden

Ver-Colne Valley Walk

River Colne

Otterspool

The Wenta
Business Cen

Capital
Business Cen

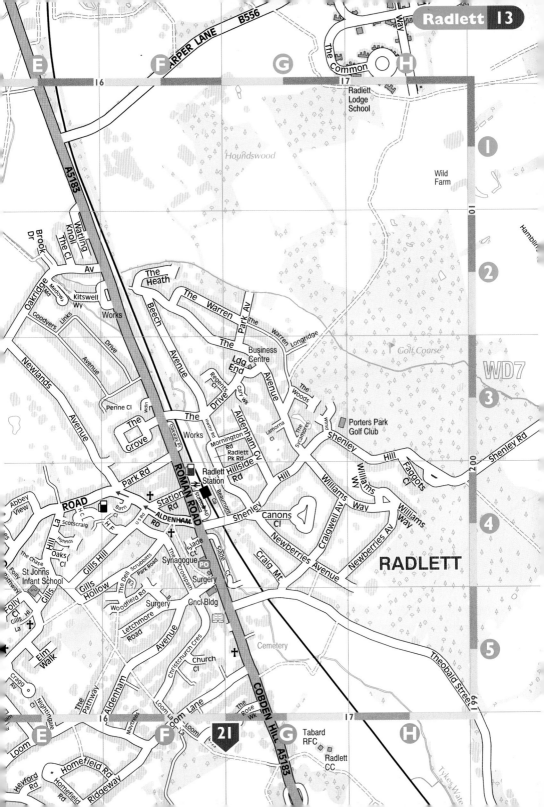

HARPER LANE B556

Way

The Common

E   16   F   G   17   H

Radlett Lodge School

I

Houndswood

Wild Farm

A5183

Watling Knoll

Brook Dr

The Cl

Av

Meadow Wy

Oakridge

Links

Goodyers

Kitswell Wy

Works

The Heath

Beech

2

The Warren

Park Av

The

The Warren

Longridge

Golf Course

WD7

Newlands

Avenue

Drive

Penne Cl

Wolvn

The Grove

Avenue

The

Business Centre

Ldg End

Regents Cl

Cary Wk

Avenue

The Woods

Golf Club

3

Drive

Works

Mornington Rd

Radlett Pk Rd

Lamorna

The Sycamores

Wstsd

Shenley

Hill

Faggots Cl

Porters Park

200

Shenley Rd

Park Rd

ROMAN ROAD

Station Rd

Radlett Station

Hillside Rd

Hill

Williams Wy

Williams Way

Williams Way

4

Abbey View

ROAD

H.C.

Barn

U's Rd

ALDENHAM RD

Scotscraig

Highlds

Beaumont

Shenley

Canons Cl

Newberries Avenue

Craigwell Av

Newberries Av

RADLETT

The Chase

Oaks Cl

H.F.

La

Gills Hill

Slade Ct

Synagogue

PO

Surgery

Craig Mt

St Johns Infant School

Folly Cl

Gills La

Gills Hollow

The Dell

Scrubbitts Park Road

Woodfield Rd

Surgery

Cncl Bldg

Cemetery

Elm Walk

Letchmore Road

Avenue

Christchurch Cres

Church Cl

Theobald Street

5

66.1

Cragg Av

Nightingale

The Pathway

Aldenham

Maytrees

Loom Lane

The Rose Wk

COBDEN Hill A5183

Heyford Rd

Homefield Rd

Loom

Ridgeway

Homefield

E   16   F   **21**   G   17   H

Tabard RFC

Radlett CC

Tykes Wate

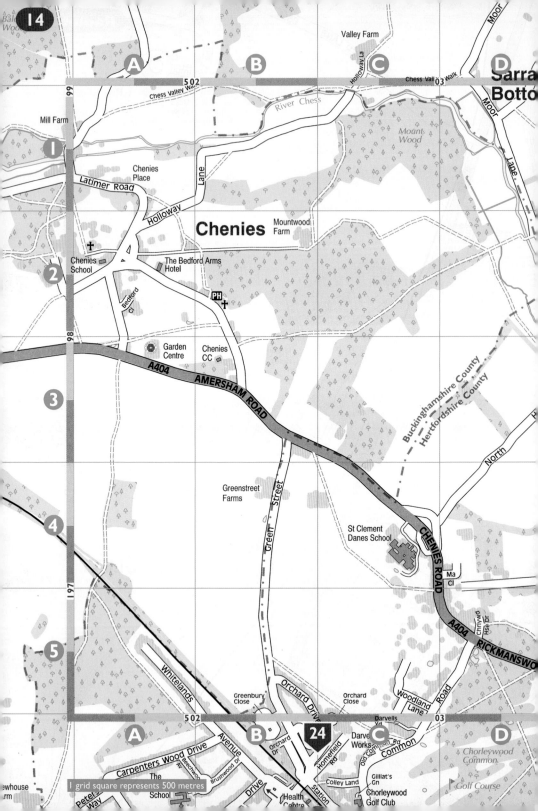

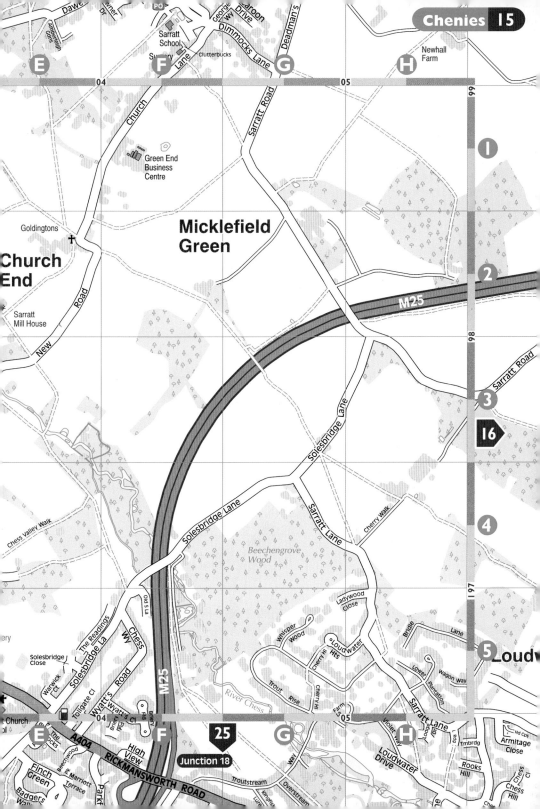

Dawe

PO

George Wy

Baroon Drive

Dimmocks Lane

Deadman's

Newhall Farm

Sarratt School

Surgery

Clutterbucks

E

F

G

H

04

05

99

I

Church

Green End Business Centre

Micklefield Green

Goldingtons

Church End

Sarratt Mill House

New Road

Road

Sarratt Road

2

M25

98

Sarratt Road

3

16

Solesbridge Lane

4

Chess Valley Walk

Solesbridge Lane

Sarratt Lane

Cherry Walk

Beechengrove Wood

Ladywood Close

197

Whisper Wood

Bridle Lane

Solesbridge Close

The Readings

Solesbridge La

Chess Wy

Old S La

Loudwater His

Cherry Hl

Lower Plantation

Wagon Way

5 Loud

Warwick Ct

Wyatt's Road

Tollgate Cl

M25

Briery Fld

Wyatt's Cl

Ladyrood

Trout Rise

Cherry Hl

Farm Ln

Sarratt Lane

Hd Cps

Church

River Chess

Violet Way

Armitage Close

E

A404

High View

F

25

Junction 18

G

H

Loudwater Drive

Rooks Hill

Chess Hill

RICKMANSWORTH ROAD

04

Briery

05

Knights

Troutstream

Overstream

Jackets

Tmbrdg

Chess Wk

Finch Green

Beechway

P Marriott Terrace

Park

Badgers

Wall

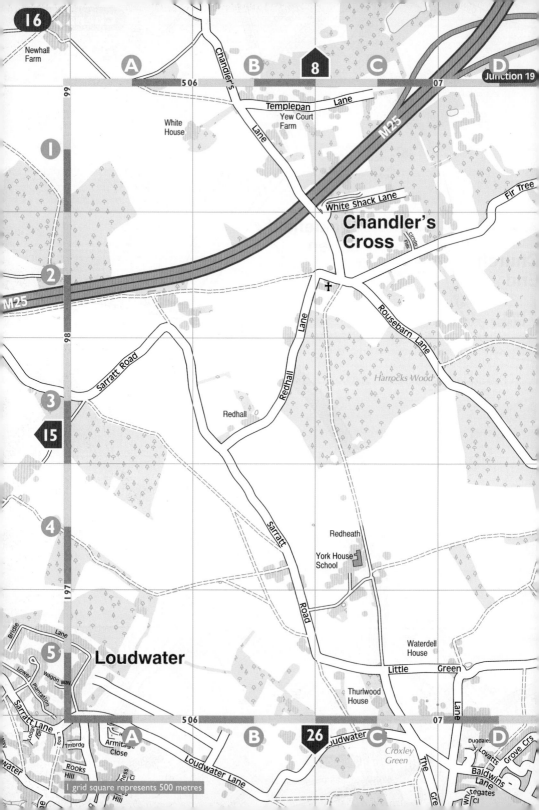

16

A   B   **8**   C   **D** Junction 19

5 06   07

Newhall Farm

I

99

White House

Chandler's Lane

Templepan Lane
Yew Court Farm

M25

White Shack Lane

Chandler's Cross

Fir Tree

2

M25

98

Redhall Lane

Rousebarn Lane

Harrocks Wood

Sarratt Road

3

I5

Redhall

4

97

Sarratt Road

Redheath

York House School

Waterdell House

5

Bridle Lane

Loudwater

Lower Plantation

Wagon way

Little Green

Thurlwood House

Lane

Sarratt Lane

A   B   **26**   C   **D**

5 06   07

Armitage Close

Loudwater Lane

Loudwater

Croxley Green

The Gre

Dugdale

Lovatts

Grove Crs

Baldwins Lane

Whitegates Cl

Rooks Hill

Tmbrdg

Lodge

Ess Cl

1 grid square represents 500 metres

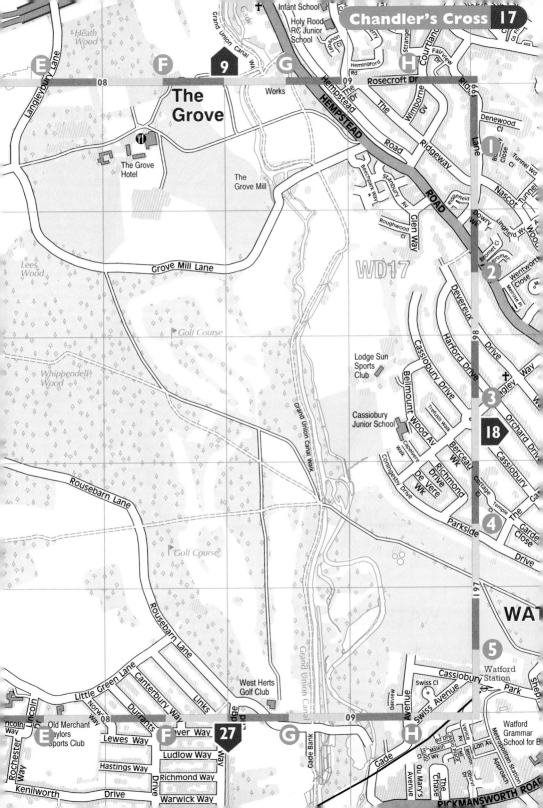

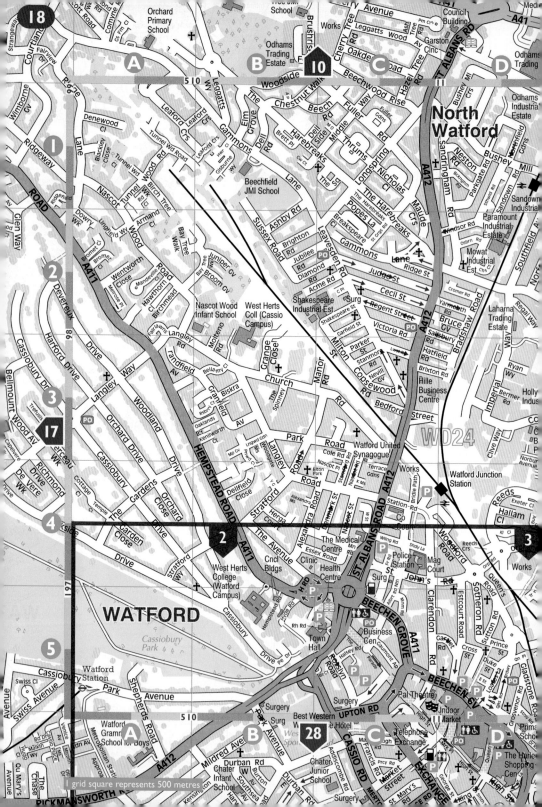

Otterspool

Aldenham

Golf Course

E

F

G

H

I

Central
Business Cen

The Wenta
Business Cen

York

PO

The
Turnstones

Way

Gadswell

Carsmouth Way

Meriden Wy

Widgeon Wy

Kelshall

Westlea Av

Eastlea Avenue

M1

Douglas Av

Tudor Walk

Tudor Avenue

Tudor Drive

Hillrise Avenue

Woodmere

Avenue

Ver-Colne Valley Walk

Stn

PO

urgery

Bushey Mill Lane

Hibber Av

Av

estfield

Rd

Busheymill
Bridge

Berry

WAY

Otterspool

Lane

GV

Lane

A41

Golf Course

Aldenham Golf
& Country Club

2

Hartspring Lane

STEPHENSON

Radlett

Road

Eastfield Av

ooke

nd Est

A4008

Bushey Mill Lane

Junction 5

Works

Otterspool

Way

Berrygrove La

M1

98

99

B462

3

20

STEPHENSON

Way

Road

Link Rd

Park Av

Highwood

Primary

School

Highwood Av

Marion
Ct

Pine

GV

The
Leas

PO

Pine

GV

Pinfold Rd

Wy

Forest
Walk

Robin Hood Dr

Friars Way

Park

Superstore

Cp House
Business Centre

Avenue

Heather

duncan way

RI

Hts

Hartspring
Sports
Centre

Hartspring
Industrial Park

4

Mead Way

Mill Way

Scottswood

Scottswood

Wd Cl

Rd

Maple
Ct

St

Park Avenue

Surgery

Bushey

Mill

Lane

Golf
Cl

Park
Cl

Link Rd

Recreation
Ground

Ver-Colne Valley Walk

River Colne

Golf Course

Queens
School

ALDENHAM

ROAD

Metropolitan Police
Bushey Sports Ground

Little Bushe

ne

Cemete

197

5

A4008

Wrks

Woolmerdiness Cl

Greatham Rd

Ashton

William

Bendysh

Walton

PO

St

Arthur
St

Bushey

Hall

Road

Greatham Road
Industrial
Estate

Bushey
Dr

Brmb

ushey Hall
olf Club

B462

29

3

Inch

Lane

E

F

G

H

A411

WATERFIE

WAY

Premier
Inn

Leonards Cl

St

Napier

Grove Hall Rd

ashton

Lambert

Premier
Inn

International
University

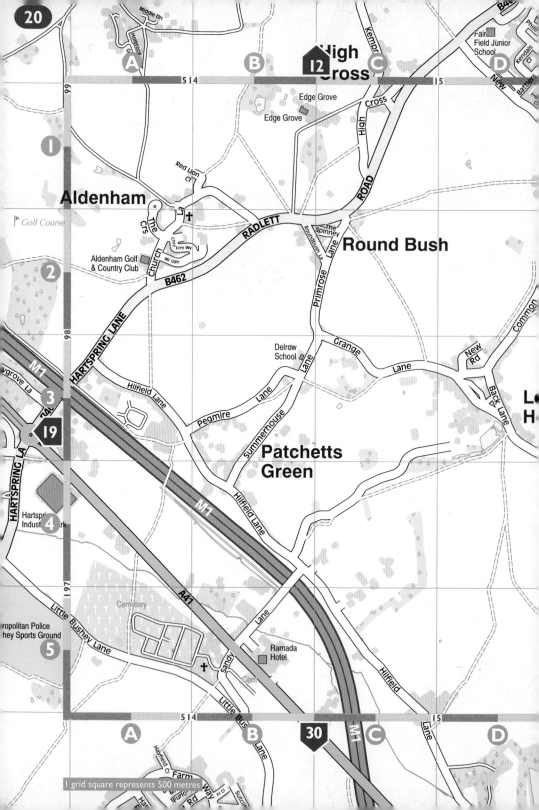

Elm Walk

Cragg Av

Christchurch Cres

Church Cl

Cemetery

E

F

13

COBDEN HILL A5183

G

H

Theobald Street

Avenue

Aldenham

The Pathway

Loom Lane

Maytrees

The Rose Wk

The Larks

Loom

Loom Lane

Tykes Water

Tabard RFC

Radlett CC

I

Heyford Rd

Homefield Rd

Homefield Rd

Ridgeway

The

Manor Ct

Loom Lane

WATLING STREET

Little Kendals Farm

Hertsmere Jewish Primary School

Radlett Preparatory School

2

98

Batlers Green

3

22

ore

Aldenham Preparatory School

Wards Lane

Slades Farm

North Medburn Farm

4

ham Road

Butterfly Lane

197

Elstree Country

Elstree Aerodrome

The Haberdashers Askes School for Boys

5

WATLING STREET

E

F

31

G

H

Water

Hogg

Lane

Dagger

Aldenham Road

Home Farm

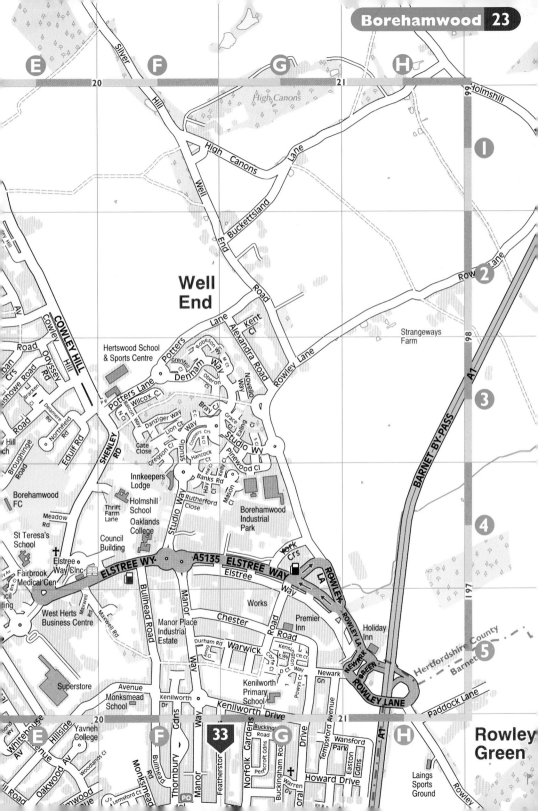

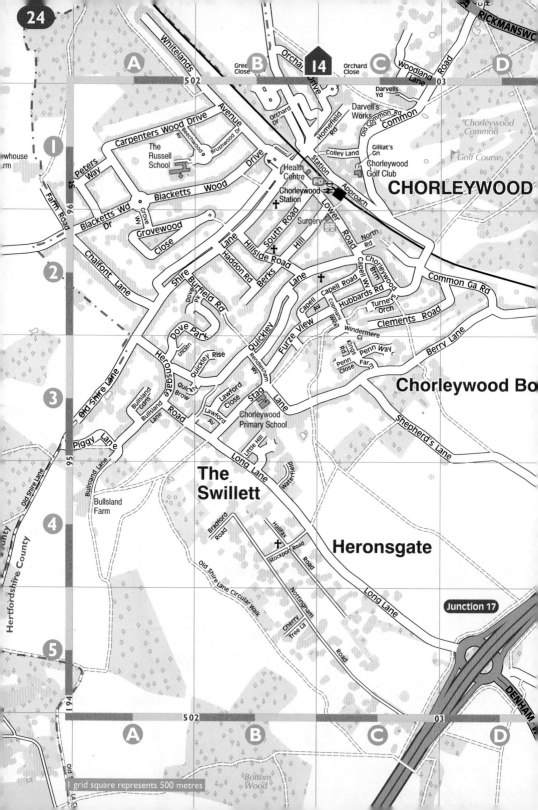

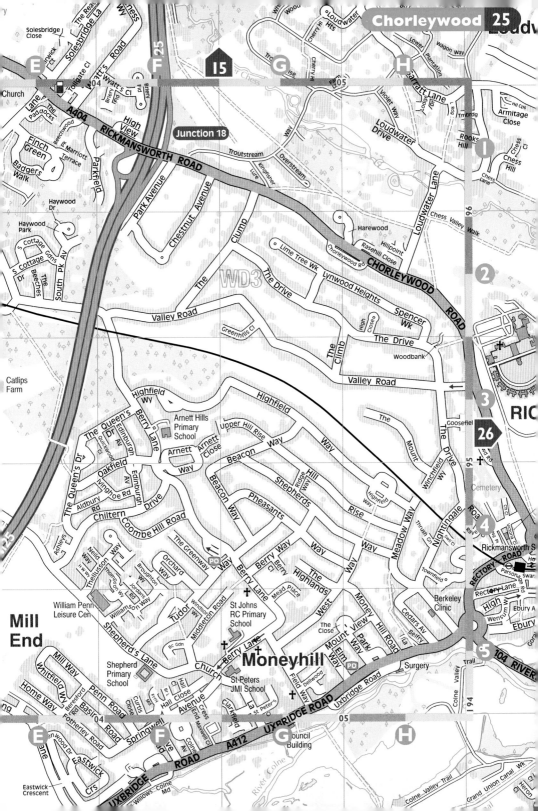

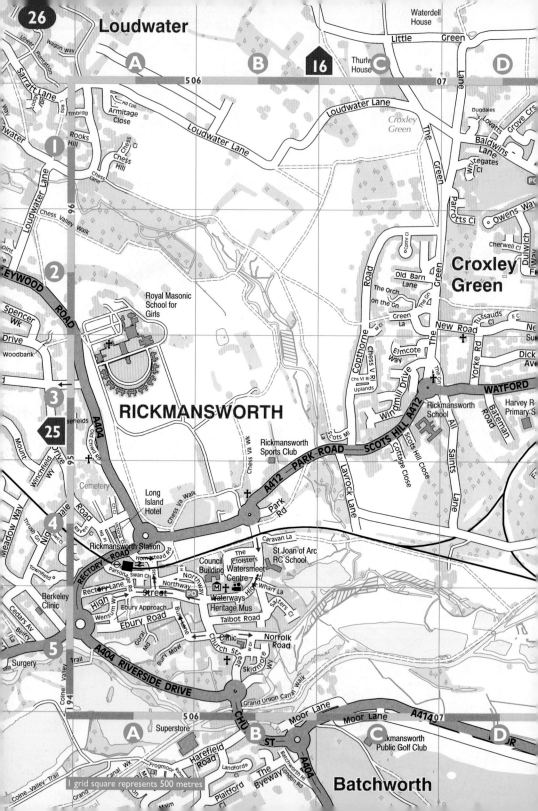

Watford Station

Cassiobury Avenue

Swiss Cl

West Herts Golf Club

I7

Little Green Lane

Norwich Way

Lincoln Dr

E

Canterbury Way

Durrants

Links

Lodge End

F

G

Gade Bank

H

Swiss Cl

Oakview

Watford Grammar School for B

Old Merchant Taylors Sports Club

Lewes Way

Dover Way

Rochester Way

Ludlow Way

Hastings Way

Richmond Way

Kenilworth Drive

Warwick Way

Baldwins Lane

Watford Metropolitan Station Approach

Cherrydale

I

The Chase

Qu Mary's Avenue

Cassiobridge Road

RICKMANSWORTH ROAD

King Georges Av

Hadden Rd

rborne Way

Winchester Way

Claremont Crs

Girton Way

Winton Ap

Dorrofield Cl

PO

Mayfare

Premier Inn

Whippendell

Gade Cl

2

Malvern Way

Lancing Way

Winton Crs

Winton

A412

Sycamore Ap

Rd

Beggars

Bush Lane

The Gateway

Sydney Road

Works

Works

Tolpits Close

Malvern Way School

Valley Walk

Sycamore

Blackmoor Lane

St Anthonys RC Primary School

Westfield Community Technology College

Springfield Cl

Beechcroft Av

The Oslers

Byewaters

Woodshots Meadow

Industrial Estate

The Blvd

Ascot Rd

Ascot Road

Croxley View

PO

Croxley Station

The Crs

Oakleigh Drive

Grand Union Canal Walk

Basildon Cl

Gill Cl

Evensyde

Heckford Cl

Hatters

Faraday Close

Greenhill

Hetters La

Gl Crs

Croxley

View

Chesham Wy

TOLF LANE

Tolpits La

Comber Road

Charl

High

3

28 School

ROAD

PO

Hazelwood Rd

Byewaters

Martins Meadow

Holywell

Croxley View

A4145

The Round Wy

ville Av

Frankland Road

Works

Crescent

Caxton Way

Latimer Cl

Chenies

Dkn Wy

Chaffinch La

4

Grand Union Canal Walk

River Gade

Moor La Crossing

Moor Park Industrial Estate

Dwight Road

Wolsey Business Park

5

Peerglow Industrial Estate

Old's Cl

Old's Ap

TOLPITS LANE

River Colne

Hampermill Lake

Byfleet Industrial Estate

MOOR LANE A4145

Vale Industrial Estate

08

09

Merchant Taylors School

194

E

Northwood Preparatory School

F

G

H

Sandy Lodge Road

East Drive

Askew Road

Wols

North

The Dell

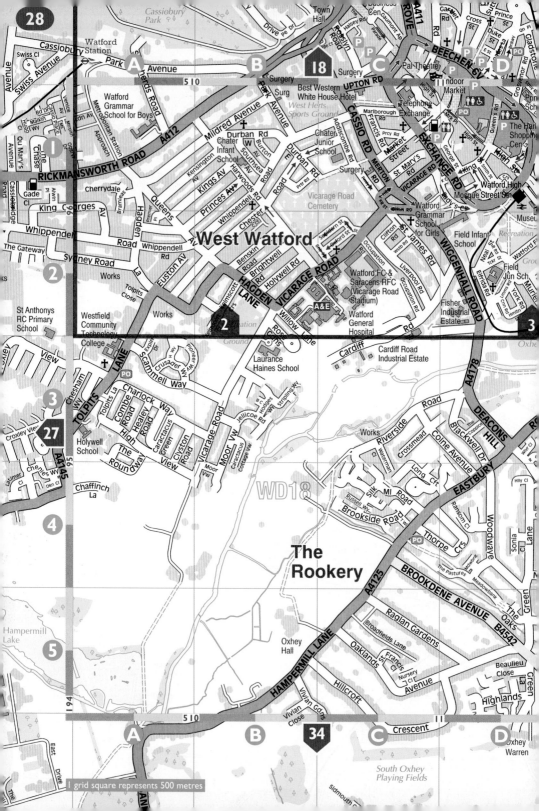

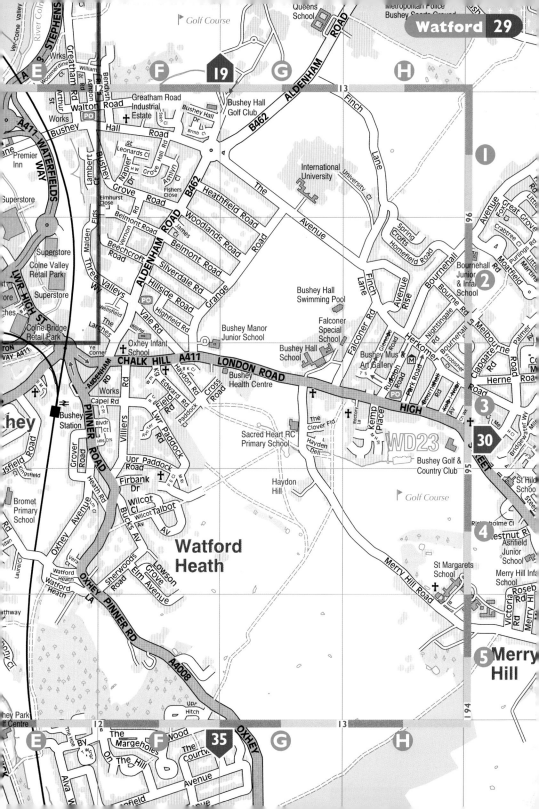

Golf Course

Queens School

Metropolitan Police Bushey Sports Ground

River Colne

STEPHENS

ST STEPHENS

E　**F**　**19**　**G**　**H**

Woolmerdine Ct

William St

Greatham Rd

Agston Rd

Walton Road

PO

Bushey Hall Road

Greatham Road Industrial Estate

Bushey Hall Golf Club

ALDENHAM ROAD

B462

B462

Finch Lane

University Ct

I

96

A411 WATERFIELDS WAY

Premier Inn

Arthur St

Lambert

St Leonards Cl

Napier Rd

H W

Grove

Hall Rd

Ashlyn

Fishers Close

Elmhurst Close

Bushey Grove Road

Heathfield Road

The Avenue

International University

Superstore

Belmont Road

Vernon Rd

Beechcroft Road

James Cl

Woodlands Road

Silverdale Rd

Belmont Road

ALDENHAM ROAD

B462

Grange

Spring Crofts

Homefield Road

Bournehall Junior & Infant School

2

Avenue Rd

Fox

Great Grove

Crabtree Ct

Purlings Rd

Martins

Moatfield Rd

Colne Valley Retail Park

Superstore

Malden Flds

Three Valleys W

Wellsfield

The Larches

PO

Hillside Road

Vale Rd

Highfield Rd

Bushey Manor Junior School

Bushey Hall Swimming Pool

Falconer Special School

Finch Lane

Avenue Rise

Herkomer Rd

Bourne Rd

Nightingale Rd

Bournehall Road

Melbourne Road

Colne Bridge Retail Park

LWR HIGH ST

Ye Corner

Oxhey Infant School

CHALK HILL A411

ALDENHAM RD

Haydon Rd

Cross Road

Bushey Health Centre

LONDON ROAD

Falconer Rd

Rudolph Road

Bushey Mus & Art Gallery

Park Road

Bushey Hall School

Glenmere

Kenilworth Dr

PO

HIGH

Clagate Rd

Herne Rd

3

30

STREET

hey

A411

Capel Rd

Bushey Station

PINNER ROAD

Villiers

Field Rd

KG

Edward Rd

LWR Paddock

Paddock Rd

Ayres Rd

Sacred Heart RC Primary School

The Clover Fld

Rectory La

Kemp Place

Bournehall Av

St Hild School

95

Grover Road

Works

Blvdr Ct

Hills Crs

Upr Paddock Road

Firbank Dr

FCD

The Clover Fld

Hayden Dell

WD23

Bushey Golf & Country Club

Risinholme Cl

4

Chestnut Rd

Ashfield Junior School

Bromet Primary School

Oxhey Avenue

Bucks Av

Wilcot Cl

Wilcot Talbot Av

Watford Heath

Haydon Hill

Golf Course

Merry Hill Road

St Margarets School

Merry Hill Infant School

Victoria Rd

Roseb Rd

Merry Hill Rd

Oxhey LA

Watford Heath

OXHEY PINNER RD

A4008

Sherwoods Road

Lowson Grove

Elm Avenue

St Margarets School

5　**Merry Hill**

194

hey Park lf Centre

Upr Hitch

E　**F**　**35**　**G**　**H**

The Margeholes

On The Hill

Nood

The Courty

OXHEY

Avenue

Alva W

The Haberdashers Askes School for Boys

Elstree Aerodrome

E **F** **21** **G** **H**

16 Aid Road 17

WATLING STREET

Hogg Lane

Dagger Lane

Tykes Water Lake

I

96

Home Farm

ilfield Park Reservoir

P Aldenham Country Park

Aldenham Road

2

Dagger Lane

Aldenham Reservoir

Lands' End

A41

M1

WATFORD ROAD

3

Robert Rd

Britten Cl

A411 ELSTREE ROAD

ELSTREE ROAD

A411

Lismarrine Industrial Park

32

Deli Cl

Beethoven

A5183

A409

Caldecote Hill

Williams Way

Elgar Close

Coates Rd

SOUTH HILL

4

South

Centennial Avenue

Centennial AV

ELSTREE HL S

A41

M1

Brockley Hill Farm

5

Junction 4

Stanmore Common

16 17

194

A5 BROCKLEY

E **F** **G** **H**

Works

Royal National Orthopaedic Hospital

Wood Lane

Nutt Gv

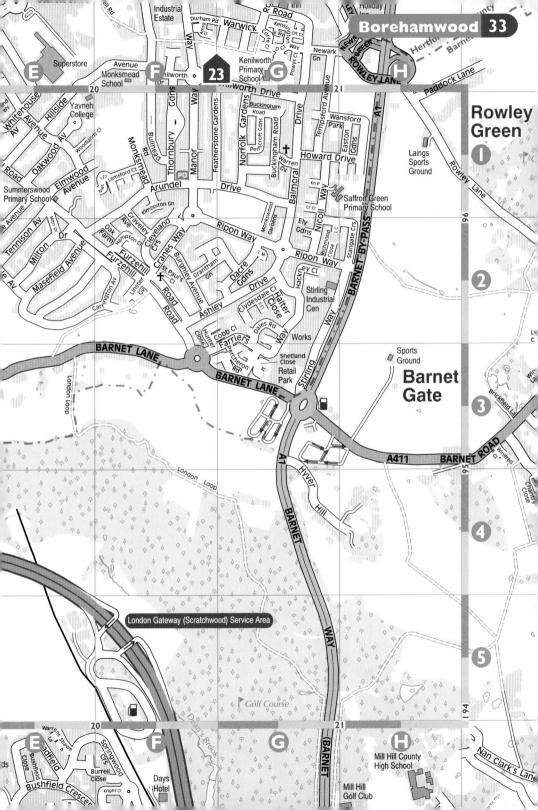

Industrial Estate

Warwick

Durham Rd

Arms Rd

Way

Road

Holiday Inn

Kenso

Cate

Ct

Kenilworth
Primary
School

Newark
Gn

NEW
GREEN

ROWLEY LANE

Hertford...
Barnet...

Paddock Lane

E Superstore

Whitehouse Avenue

Hillside

Yavneh College

Avenue
Monksmead School

F Kenilworth

Dr

23

Kenilworth Drive

G

H

20

21

A1

Rowley Green

1

Oakwood Road

Elmwood Avenue

Summerswood Primary School

Monksmead Rd

Bullhead Rd

Thornbury Gdns

Featherstone Gardens

Manor

Way

Norfolk Gardens

Buckingham Road

Buckingham Road

Pets-croft Gdns

Balmoral

Howard Drive

Tempsford Avenue

Drive

Wansford Park

Easton Gdns

Laings Sports Ground

Rowley Lane

96

PO

Arundel

Drive

Warren Gv

Saffron Green Primary School

Kn P

NICOL Way

Cr Cl

Cr Cl

Tennison Av

Milton Av

Masefield Avenue

Graveley Ave

Oak Farm

Hampton Cl

Kimbolton Gn

Cleveland Crs

Cranes Way

St Paul's

Burghley Avenue

Grantham Gn

Ripon Way

Ripon Way

Monkswood Gardens

Ely Gdns

Stangate Crs

Richmond Close

2

Furzehill

Furzehill Road

Linster Gv

Carrington Av

Dacre Gdns

Ashley

Drive

Hatter Close

Way

Clydesdale Cl

Dales Rd

Hackney Cl

Stirling Industrial Cen

Barnet By-Pass

BARNET LANE

BARNET LANE

Hunter Cl

Cobb Cl

Farriers

Percheron Way

Shetland Close

Retail Park

Works

Stirling Way

Sports Ground

Barnet Gate

3

Brickfield La

London Loop

London Loop

A1

BARNET

WAY

Hyver Hill

A411 **BARNET ROAD**

Winifred Cl

Chartley Close

95

4

London Gateway (Scratchwood) Service Area

5

194

Golf Course

Dean's Brook

20

21

BARNET

E

Warren Shaw La

Leadfield Close

Bushfield Close

Springwood Close

Burrell Close

Bushfield Crescent

Knight Cl

F

Days Hotel

G

H

Mill Hill County High School

Mill Hill Golf Club

Nan Clark's La

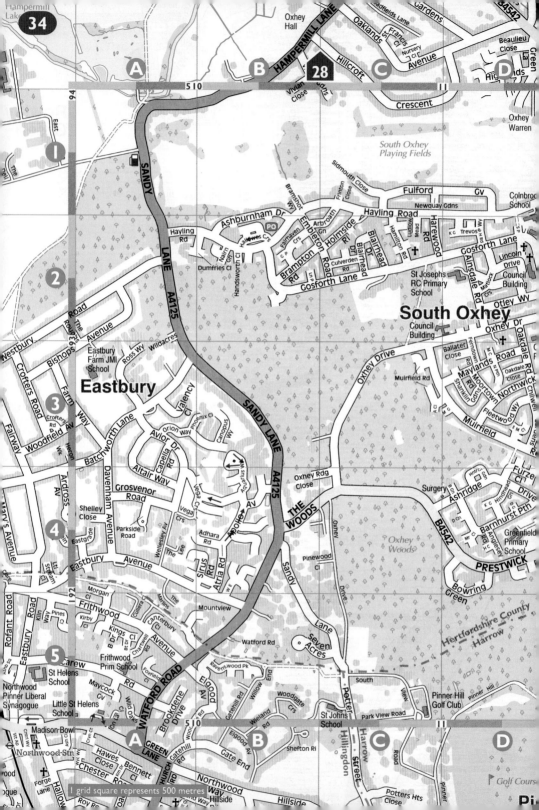

Abbots Langley	9 H1	Church End	15 E2	Leavesden Green	9 H3	Round Bush	20
Aldenham	20 A1	Croxley Green	26 D2	Letchmore Heath	20 D3	South Oxhey	34
Barnet Gate	33 H3	Deacons Hill	32 D3	Loudwater	16 A5	The Swillett	24
Batlers Green	21 E2	Eastbury	34 A3	Meriden	11 F5	Waterdale	6
Bedmond	5 H1	Elstree	32 B3	Merry Hill	30 A5	Watford	3
Borehamwood	22 B5	Garston	10 D4	Micklefield Green	15 F2	Watford Heath	29
Bricket Wood	7 G5	Green Street	22 D1	Mill End	25 E5	Well End	23
Bushey	30 B4	The Grove	17 F1	Moneyhill	25 G5	West Watford	2
Bushey Heath	30 D4	Heronsgate	24 C4	North Watford	18 C1	Woodside	10
Caldecote Hill	31 E4	High Cross	12 C5	Otterspool	19 G1		
Carpenders Park	35 G1	Holywell	27 H3	Oxhey	29 E3		
Chandler's Cross	16 C2	Hunton Bridge	9 E2	Patchetts Green	20 B3		
Chenies	14 B2	Kings Langley	4 D2	Radlett	13 H4		
Chorleywood	24 C1	Kingswood	10 D4	Rickmansworth	26 A3		
Chorleywood Bottom	24 C3	Langleybury	9 E3	The Rookery	28 B4		

USING THE STREET INDEX

Street names are listed alphabetically. Each street name is followed by its postal town or area locality, the Postcode District, the page number, and the reference to the square in which the name is found.

Standard index entries are shown as follows:

Abbey Dr *ABLGY* WD5....................**10** B1

Street names and selected addresses not shown on the map due to scale restrictions are shown in the index with an asterisk:

Albany Ms *LCOL/BKTW* AL2 *..........**7** H1

GENERAL ABBREVIATIONS

ACC	ACCESS	EXPY	EXPRESSWAY	MI	MILL
ALY	ALLEY	EXT	EXTENSION	MKT	MARKET
AP	APPROACH	F/O	FLYOVER	MKTS	MARKETS
AR	ARCADE	FC	FOOTBALL CLUB	ML	MALL
ASS	ASSOCIATION	FK	FORK	MNR	MANOR
AV	AVENUE	FLD	FIELD	MS	MEWS
BCH	BEACH	FLDS	FIELDS	MSN	MISSION
BLDS	BUILDINGS	FLS	FALLS	MT	MOUNT
BND	BEND	FM	FARM	MTN	MOUNTAIN
BNK	BANK	FT	FORT	MTS	MOUNTAINS
BR	BRIDGE	FTS	FLATS	MUS	MUSEUM
BRK	BROOK	FWY	FREEWAY	MWY	MOTORWAY
BTM	BOTTOM	FY	FERRY	N	NORTH
BUS	BUSINESS	GA	GATE	NE	NORTH EAST
BVD	BOULEVARD	GAL	GALLERY	NW	NORTH WEST
BY	BYPASS	GDN	GARDEN	O/P	OVERPASS
CATH	CATHEDRAL	GDNS	GARDENS	OFF	OFFICE
CEM	CEMETERY	GLD	GLADE	ORCH	ORCHARD
CFT	CROFT	GLN	GLEN	OV	OVAL
CH	CHURCH	GN	GREEN	PAL	PALACE
CHA	CHASE	GND	GROUND	PAS	PASSAGE
CHYD	CHURCHYARD	GRA	GRANGE	PAV	PAVILION
CIR	CIRCLE	GRG	GARAGE	PDE	PARADE
CIRC	CIRCUS	GT	GREAT	PH	PUBLIC HOUSE
CL	CLOSE	GTWY	GATEWAY	PK	PARK
CLFS	CLIFFS	GV	GROVE	PKWY	PARKWAY
CMP	CAMP	HGR	HIGHER	PL	PLACE
CNR	CORNER	HL	HILL	PLN	PLAIN
CO	COUNTY	HLS	HILLS	PLNS	PLAINS
COLL	COLLEGE	HO	HOUSE	PLZ	PLAZA
COM	COMMON	HOL	HOLLOW	POL	POLICE STATION
COMM	COMMISSION	HOSP	HOSPITAL	PR	PRINCE
CON	CONVENT	HRB	HARBOUR	PREC	PRECINCT
COT	COTTAGE	HTH	HEATH	PREP	PREPARATORY
COTS	COTTAGES	HTS	HEIGHTS	PRIM	PRIMARY
CP	CAPE	HVN	HAVEN	PROM	PROMENADE
CPS	COPSE	HWY	HIGHWAY	PRS	PRINCESS
CR	CREEK	IMP	IMPERIAL	PRT	PORT
CREM	CREMATORIUM	IN	INLET	PT	POINT
CRS	CRESCENT	IND EST	INDUSTRIAL ESTATE	PTH	PATH
CSWY	CAUSEWAY	INF	INFIRMARY	PZ	PIAZZA
CT	COURT	INFO	INFORMATION	QD	QUADRANT
CTRL	CENTRAL	INT	INTERCHANGE	QU	QUEEN
CTS	COURTS	IS	ISLAND	QY	QUAY
CTYD	COURTYARD	JCT	JUNCTION	R	RIVER
CUTT	CUTTINGS	JTY	JETTY	RBT	ROUNDABOUT
CV	COVE	KG	KING	RD	ROAD
CYN	CANYON	KNL	KNOLL	RDG	RIDGE
DEPT	DEPARTMENT	L	LAKE	REP	REPUBLIC
DL	DALE	LA	LANE	RES	RESERVOIR
DM	DAM	LDG	LODGE	RFC	RUGBY FOOTBALL CLUB
DR	DRIVE	LGT	LIGHT	RI	RISE
DRO	DROVE	LK	LOCK	RP	RAMP
DRY	DRIVEWAY	LKS	LAKES	RW	ROW
DWGS	DWELLINGS	LNDG	LANDING	S	SOUTH
E	EAST	LTL	LITTLE	SCH	SCHOOL
EMB	EMBANKMENT	LWR	LOWER	SE	SOUTH EAST
EMBY	EMBASSY	MAG	MAGISTRATES'	SER	SERVICE AREA
ESP	ESPLANADE	MAN	MANSIONS	SH	SHORE
EST	ESTATE	MD	MEAD	SHOP	SHOPPING
EX	EXCHANGE	MDW	MEADOWS	SKWY	SKYWAY
		MEM	MEMORIAL	SMT	SUMMIT

SOC	SOCI...
SP	SP...
SPR	SPR...
SQ	SQU...
ST	STR...
STN	STAT...
STR	STRE...
STRD	STRA...
SW	SOUTH W...
TDG	TRAD...
TER	TERR...
THWY	THROUGHW...
TNL	TUN...
TOLL	TOLLW...
TPK	TURNP...
TR	TRA...
TRL	TR...
TWR	TWR...
U/P	UNDERP...
UNI	UNIVERS...
UPR	UPP...
V	V...
VA	VAL...
VIAD	VIAD...
VIL	VI...
VIS	VI...
VLG	VILL...
VLS	VIL...
VW	V...
W	W...
WD	WC...
WHF	WHA...
WK	W...
WKS	WA...
WLS	WE...
WY	WY...
YD	YA...
YHA	YOUTH HOS...

POSTCODE TOWNS AND AREA ABBREVIATIONS

ABLGY	Abbots Langley	HHS/BOV	Hemel Hempstead south/ Bovingdon	LCOL/BKTW	London Colney/ Bricket Wood
BAR	Barnet				
BORE	Borehamwood	KGLGY	Kings Langley	MLHL	Mill Hill
BUSH	Bushey	KTN/HRWW/WS	Kenton/ Harrow Weald/ Wealdstone	NTHWD	Northwood
CSTG	Chalfont St Giles			OXHEY	Oxhey
EDGW	Edgware			PIN	Pinner
GSTN	Garston			RAD	Radlett

RKW/CH/CXG	Rickmanswor... Chorleywo... Croxley Gre...
STAN	Stanmo...
WAT	Watfo...
WATN	Watford no...
WATW	Watford w...

Catsey Wd *BUSH* WD23 .... 30 B4
Catterick Wy *BORE* WD6 .... 22 C3
Cavendish Ct
  RKW/CH/CXG WD3 * 27 G2
Cavendish Crs *BORE* WD6 .... 32 D1
Caxton Wy *WATW* WD18 .... 27 G4
Cecil St *WATN* WD24 .... 18 C2
Cedar Dr *PIN* HA5 .... 35 H5
Cedar Rd *OXHEY* WD19 .... 28 D3
Cedars Av *RKW/CH/CXG* WD3 ...... 25 H5
Cedars Cl *BORE* WD6 .... 23 F2
Cedar Wood Dr *GSTN* WD25 .... 10 C4
Centennial Av *BORE* WD6 .... 31 G4
Centennial Pk *BORE* WD6 * 31 H4
Century Ct *WATW* WD18 * 27 F4
Century Pk *WAT* WD17 * 3 H7
Chaffinch La *WATW* WD18 .... 27 H3
Chalfont La *RKW/CH/CXG* WD3 .... 24 A2
Chalk Hl *OXHEY* WD19 .... 29 F3
Champions Cl *BORE* WD6 .... 23 E1
Champneys *OXHEY* WD19 * 35 E1
Chandler's La
  RKW/CH/CXG WD3 .... 8 B5
Chandos Rd *BORE* WD6 .... 22 C4
Chantry Cl *KGLGY* WD4 .... 4 D3
Chapel Cl *BUSH* WD23 .... 10 A3
Chapel Wy *ABLGY* WD5 .... 6 A1
Chapmans Yd *WAT* WD17 * 3 H5
Charlock Wy *WATW* WD18 .... 28 A3
Charter Pl *WAT* WD17 * 3 F3
Chartridge *OXHEY* WD19 * 35 E1
Chartridge Cl *BUSH* WD23 .... 30 B3
Chartwell Rd *NTHWD* HA6 .... 34 A5
The Chase *WAT* WD7 .... 13 E4
  WATW WD18 .... 27 H1
Chatsworth Rd *BORE* WD6 .... 22 D5
Chenies Rd *RKW/CH/CXG* WD3 .... 14 C4
Chenies Wy *WATW* WD18 .... 27 H4
Chequers La *GSTN* WD25 .... 6 C4
Cherry Cft *RKW/CH/CXG* WD3 ..... 26 D5
Cherrydale *WATW* WD18 .... 2 A5
Cherry Hl *RKW/CH/CXG* WD3 .... 5 G5
Cherry Hills *OXHEY* WD19 .... 35 F4
Cherry Hollow *ABLGY* WD5 .... 6 A5
Cherry Tree La
  RKW/CH/CXG WD3 .... 24 B5
Cherry Tree Rd *WATN* WD24 .... 18 D2
Cherry Wk *RKW/CH/CXG* WD3 ...... 15 H4
Cherwell Cl *RKW/CH/CXG* WD3 .... 26 D2
Chesham Wy *WATW* WD18 .... 27 H3
Cheshire Dr *GSTN* WD25 .... 10 A3
Chess Cl *RKW/CH/CXG* WD3 .... 26 A1
Chess Hl *RKW/CH/CXG* WD3 .... 26 A1
Chess La *RKW/CH/CXG* WD3 .... 26 A1
Chess Vale Ri *RKW/CH/CXG* WD3 . 26 B3
Chess Wy *RKW/CH/CXG* WD3 .... 15 F5
Chesswood Ct
  RKW/CH/CXG WD3 * 26 A5
Chester Rd *BORE* WD6 .... 23 F5
  WATW WD18 .... 2 C6
Chestnut Av *RKW/CH/CXG* WD3 .. 25 F2
Chestnut Ri *BUSH* WD23 .... 30 A4
Chestnut Wk *WATN* WD24 .... 18 B1
Cheviot St *BUSH* WD23 .... 30 B3
Cheyne Ct *BUSH* WD23 .... 29 F1
Chichester Wy *GSTN* WD25 .... 11 F2
Chilcott Rd *WATN* WD24 .... 9 H5
Chiltern Av *BUSH* WD23 .... 30 B3
Chiltern Cl *BORE* WD6 .... 22 C4
  BUSH WD23 .... 30 A4
Chiltern Dr *RKW/CH/CXG* WD3 ... 25 E4
Chiltern Est *WATN* WD24 * 18 D3
Chilwell Gdns *OXHEY* WD19 .... 34 D3
Chipperfield Rd *KGLGY* WD4 .... 4 A3
Chiswell Ct *WATN* WD24 .... 18 D2
Chorleywood Bottom
  RKW/CH/CXG WD3 .... 24 C2
Chorleywood Cl
  RKW/CH/CXG WD3 .... 26 A4
Chorleywood House Dr
  RKW/CH/CXG WD3 .... 14 D5
Chorleywood Rd
  RKW/CH/CXG WD3 .... 25 G2
Christchurch Crs *RAD* WD7 .... 13 F5
Christie Ct *WATW* WD18 .... 2 C6
Church Cl *RAD* WD7 .... 13 F5
Church Farm Wy *GSTN* WD25 ...... 20 A2
Church Flds *RAD* WD7 * 13 F5
Church La *GSTN* WD25 .... 4 D4
  KGLGY WD4 .... 4 D4
  RKW/CH/CXG WD3 .... 15 F1
  RKW/CH/CXG WD3 .... 25 F5
Church Rd *WAT* WD17 .... 18 B3
Church St *RKW/CH/CXG* WD3 ...... 26 B5
  WATW WD18 .... 3 G5
Church Wk *BUSH* WD23 .... 29 H3
Clapgate Rd *BUSH* WD23 .... 30 A3
Clare Cl *BORE* WD6 .... 32 C3
Claremont *LCOL/BKTW* AL2 .... 7 H5
Claremont Crs
  RKW/CH/CXG WD3 .... 27 F2
Claremont House *WATW* WD18 * .. 27 G3
Clarence Cl *BUSH* WD23 .... 31 E4
Clarendon Flds
  RKW/CH/CXG WD3 .... 16 C2
Clarendon Ms *BORE* WD6 * 22 D5
Clarendon Rd *BORE* WD6 .... 22 D5
  WAT WD17 .... 3 F1
  WAT WD17 .... 3 F1
Clarke Gn *GSTN* WD25 .... 10 B4
Clarke Wy *GSTN* WD25 .... 10 B4

Clarkfield *RKW/CH/CXG* WD3 ..... 25 F5
Clarks Md *BUSH* WD23 .... 30 B4
Claybury *BUSH* WD23 .... 30 A4
Clay La *BUSH* WD23 .... 30 D4
Clements Rd *RKW/CH/CXG* WD3 . 24 C2
Cleveland Crs *BORE* WD6 .... 33 F2
Clifton Rd *WATW* WD18 .... 3 F6
Clifton Wy *BORE* WD6 .... 22 D3
The Climb *RKW/CH/CXG* WD3 ..... 25 G3
Clitheroe Gdns *OXHEY* WD19 ..... 35 E2
Clive Wy *WATN* WD24 .... 18 D3
Clockhouse Ms
  RKW/CH/CXG WD3 * 14 D5
The Cloisters *RKW/CH/CXG* WD3 . 26 B4
Clonard Wy *PIN* HA5 .... 35 H5
The Close *BUSH* WD23 * 29 H3
  RAD WD7 .... 13 E2
  RKW/CH/CXG WD3 .... 25 G5
The Clover Fld *BUSH* WD23 .... 29 G3
The Clump *RKW/CH/CXG* WD3 ..... 25 F2
Clydesdale Cl *BUSH* WD23 .... 30 C2
Clydesdale Pth *BORE* WD6 * 33 G2
Clyston Rd *WATW* WD18 .... 28 A5
Coates Dell *GSTN* WD25 .... 11 F2
Coates Rd *BORE* WD6 .... 32 A4
Coates Wy *GSTN* WD25 .... 11 E2
Cobb Cl *BORE* WD6 .... 33 F2
Cobb Gn *GSTN* WD25 .... 10 C1
Cobden Hl *RAD* WD7 .... 13 G5
Codicote Dr *GSTN* WD25 .... 11 E3
Colburn Av *PIN* HA5 .... 35 F5
Coldharbour La *BUSH* WD23 .... 30 A3
Coleridge Wy *BORE* WD6 .... 32 D1
Cole Rd *WAT* WD17 .... 18 C3
Coles Gn *BUSH* WD23 .... 30 B5
College Rd *ABLGY* WD5 .... 6 B5
Colley Land *RKW/CH/CXG* WD3 .. 24 C1
Colne Av *OXHEY* WD19 .... 28 C3
Colne Ldg *BUSH* WD23 * 3 K4
Colne Way Ct *WATN* WD24 * 19 E1
Colonial Wy *WATN* WD24 .... 18 D3
Combe Rd *WATW* WD18 .... 28 A3
Comet Cl *GSTN* WD25 .... 10 A3
Common Gate Rd
  RKW/CH/CXG WD3 .... 24 C2
Common La *GSTN* WD25 .... 20 D2
  KGLGY WD4 .... 4 C2
Common Rd *RKW/CH/CXG* WD3 .. 24 C1
The Common
  RKW/CH/CXG WD3 * 24 D2
Community Wy
  RKW/CH/CXG WD3 .... 26 D2
Compton Pl *OXHEY* WD19 .... 35 F3
Comyne Rd *WATN* WD24 .... 10 A5
The Comyns *BUSH* WD23 .... 30 B5
The Conifers *GSTN* WD25 .... 10 D4
Coningesby Dr *WAT* WD17 .... 17 H3
Coningsby Ct *RAD* WD7 * 13 F5
Coniston Rd *KGLGY* WD4 .... 4 C2
Connemara Cl *BORE* WD6 * 33 F3
Cooks Md *BUSH* WD23 .... 30 A3
Coombe Hill Rd
  RKW/CH/CXG WD3 .... 25 F4
Coombe Rd *BUSH* WD23 .... 30 B4
Coopers Crs *BORE* WD6 .... 23 F3
Copmans Wick
  RKW/CH/CXG WD3 .... 24 C2
The Coppice *OXHEY* WD19 .... 28 D3
Copsewood Rd *WATN* WD24 .... 18 C3
Copthorne Cl *RKW/CH/CXG* WD3 26 C2
Copthorne Rd
  RKW/CH/CXG WD3 .... 26 C3
Corfe Cl *BORE* WD6 .... 23 G5
Cornfield Rd *BUSH* WD23 .... 30 A1
Cotswold Av *BUSH* WD23 .... 30 B3
Cottage Cl *RKW/CH/CXG* WD3 .... 26 C3
  WAT WD17 .... 18 A4
Courtlands Cl *WATN* WD24 .... 9 H4
Courtlands Dr *WAT* WD17 .... 9 H5
The Courtway *OXHEY* WD19 .... 35 F1
The Courtyards *WATW* WD18 * 27 G4
Cow La *BUSH* WD23 * 29 H3
  GSTN WD25 .... 10 A4
Cowley Hl *BORE* WD6 .... 22 D1
  BORE WD6 .... 23 E2
Cowper Ct *WATN* WD24 .... 18 B1
Crab La *GSTN* WD25 .... 12 A3
Crabtree Cl *BUSH* WD23 .... 30 A2
Cragg Av *RAD* WD7 .... 13 E5
Craig Mt *RAD* WD7 .... 13 G4
Craigweil Av *RAD* WD7 .... 13 G4
Crakers Md *WATW* WD18 * 2 C4
Cranefield Dr *GSTN* WD25 .... 11 F1
Cranes Wy *BORE* WD6 .... 33 F2
Creasy Cl *ABLGY* WD5 .... 6 A5
The Crescent *ABLGY* WD5 .... 6 A4
  GSTN WD25 .... 20 A2
  LCOL/BKTW AL2 .... 7 H4
  RKW/CH/CXG WD3 .... 27 E3
  WATW WD18 .... 3 G5
Cress End *RKW/CH/CXG* WD3 ..... 25 F5
Croft Ct *BORE* WD6 .... 23 G5
Cromer Rd *WATN* WD24 .... 18 D2
Cromwell Rd *BORE* WD6 .... 22 B3
Crossmead *OXHEY* WD19 .... 28 C3
The Crosspath *RAD* WD7 .... 13 F4
Cross Oak *OXHEY* WD19 .... 29 F3
Cross St *WAT* WD17 .... 3 F3
Crowborough Pth *OXHEY* WD19 .. 35 E3
Crown Ri *GSTN* WD25 .... 10 D3
Crown Rd *BORE* WD6 .... 23 G3

Croxdale Rd *BORE* WD6 .... 22 C4
Croxley Vw *WATW* WD18 .... 27 H3
Crusader Wy *WATW* WD18 .... 28 A3
Cuffley Av *GSTN* WD25 .... 11 E3
Cullera Cl *NTHWD* HA6 .... 34 A5
Culverden Rd *OXHEY* WD19 .... 34 C2
Curtis Cl *RKW/CH/CXG* WD3 .... 25 F5
Curtiss Dr *GSTN* WD25 .... 10 A3
Cygnet Cl *BORE* WD6 .... 23 F3
Cypress Wk *GSTN* WD25 * 10 C4

D

Dacre Gdns *BORE* WD6 .... 33 G2
Dagger La *BORE* WD6 .... 31 F1
Dairy Wy *ABLGY* WD5 .... 6 A3
Dale Ct *GSTN* WD25 * 10 B2
Dales Pth *BORE* WD6 * 33 G2
Dales Rd *BORE* WD6 .... 33 G2
Dalton Wy *WAT* WD17 .... 29 E5
Danziger Wy *BORE* WD6 .... 23 F3
Darrington Rd *BORE* WD6 .... 22 B3
Darvells Yd *RKW/CH/CXG* WD3 ... 24 C1
Darwin Gdns *OXHEY* WD19 .... 34 D4
Davenham Av *NTHWD* HA6 .... 34 A3
Deacons Cl *BORE* WD6 .... 32 D1
Deacons Hts *BORE* WD6 .... 32 D3
Deacons Hl *OXHEY* WD19 .... 28 D3
  WATW WD18 .... 28 D3
Deacon's Hill Rd *BORE* WD6 .... 32 C2
Deakin Cl *WATW* WD18 .... 27 H4
Dean Ct *GSTN* WD25 * 11 E2
Deans Cl *ABLGY* WD5 .... 9 G1
De Havilland Wy *ABLGY* WD5 ...... 10 A1
Delamere Rd *BORE* WD6 .... 23 G3
Delius Cl *BORE* WD6 .... 31 H3
Dellfield Cl *RAD* WD7 .... 12 D4
  WAT WD17 .... 18 B4
Dellmeadow *ABLGY* WD5 .... 5 H4
Dell Cl *WATN* WD24 .... 18 B1
Dell Side *WATN* WD24 .... 18 B1
The Dell *RAD* WD7 .... 13 F5
Dellwood *RKW/CH/CXG* WD3 ...... 25 G5
Delta Gain *OXHEY* WD19 .... 35 E1
Denewood Cl *WAT* WD17 .... 18 A1
Denham Av *BORE* WD6 .... 23 F3
Denham Wy (North Orbital Rd)
  RKW/CH/CXG WD3 .... 24 D5
Denmark St *WAT* WD17 .... 3 H3
Derby Rd *WAT* WD17 .... 3 H4
Derwent Av *PIN* HA5 .... 35 F5
Derwent Cl *GSTN* WD25 .... 10 D2
Desmond Rd *WATN* WD24 .... 10 A5
Devereux Dr *WAT* WD17 .... 17 H2
De Vere Wk *WAT* WD17 .... 17 H4
Devon Rd *WATN* WD24 .... 19 E3
Dharam Marg *GSTN* WD25 * 20 B2
Diamond Rd *WATN* WD24 .... 18 B2
Dickinson Av *RKW/CH/CXG* WD3 . 26 D3
Dickinson Sq *RKW/CH/CXG* WD3 26 D3
Digswell Cl *BORE* WD6 .... 22 D2
Dog Kennel La
  RKW/CH/CXG WD3 .... 25 E1
Doncaster Gn *OXHEY* WD19 .... 34 D4
Dorchester Ct
  RKW/CH/CXG WD3 * 27 F2
Dorrofield Cl *RKW/CH/CXG* WD3 . 27 F2
Douglas Av *WATN* WD24 .... 19 E1
Dove Pk *RKW/CH/CXG* WD3 .... 24 A3
Dover Wy *RKW/CH/CXG* WD3 ...... 27 F2
Dowding Wy *GSTN* WD25 .... 10 A3
Downalong *BUSH* WD23 .... 30 C5
Dowry Wk *WAT* WD17 .... 17 H2
Drayton Rd *BORE* WD6 .... 32 D1
The Drive *RAD* WD7 .... 13 F3
  RKW/CH/CXG WD3 .... 25 G2
  WAT WD17 .... 17 G1
Drop La *LCOL/BKTW* AL2 .... 12 C1
Dugdales *RKW/CH/CXG* WD3 ...... 26 D1
Duke St *WAT* WD17 .... 3 G3
Dulwich Wy *RKW/CH/CXG* WD3 .. 26 D2
Dumfries Cl *OXHEY* WD19 .... 34 B2
Duncan Wy *BUSH* WD23 .... 19 G4
Dunnock Cl *BORE* WD6 .... 32 D1
Dunsmore *OXHEY* WD19 * 35 E1
Dunsmore Cl *BUSH* WD23 .... 30 D3
Dunsmore Wy *BUSH* WD23 .... 30 B3
Dunster Ct *BORE* WD6 .... 23 G5
Durban Rd East *WATN* WD18 .... 2 C4
Durban Rd West *WATN* WD18 .... 2 C4
Durham Rd *BORE* WD6 .... 23 F5
Durrants Dr *RKW/CH/CXG* WD3 .. 17 F5
Dwight Rd *WATW* WD18 .... 27 G4
Dylan Cl *BORE* WD6 * 32 A4

E

Ealing Cl *BORE* WD6 .... 23 G3
Earl St *WAT* WD17 .... 3 G3
Eastbury Ct *OXHEY* WD19 * 28 D4
Eastbury Rd *OXHEY* WD19 .... 28 D4
East Dr *GSTN* WD25 .... 10 C5
Eastfield Av *WATN* WD24 .... 19 E3
East La *ABLGY* WD5 .... 6 A3
Eastlea Av *GSTN* WD25 .... 19 F1
Easton Gdns *BORE* WD6 .... 33 H1
Eaton Wy *BORE* WD6 .... 22 C3

Ebury Ap *RKW/CH/CXG* WD3 ....
Ebury Rd *RKW/CH/CXG* WD3 ....
  WAT WD17 ....
Edgwarebury La *BORE* WD6 ....
  EDGW HA8 ....
Edinburgh Av
  RKW/CH/CXG WD3 ....
Edinburgh Dr *ABLGY* WD5 ....
Edmund Ms *KGLGY* WD4 ....
Edridge Cl *BUSH* WD23 ....
Edulf Rd *BORE* WD6 ....
Edward Amey Cl *GSTN* WD25 .....
Edward Cl *ABLGY* WD5 ....
Egg Farm La *KGLGY* WD4 ....
Elderberry Wy *GSTN* WD25 ....
Eldon Av *BORE* WD6 ....
Elfrida Rd *WATW* WD18 ....
Elgar Cl *BORE* WD6 ....
Elgood Av *NTHWD* HA6 ....
Ellenbrook Cl *WATN* WD24 * ....
Ellesborough Cl *OXHEY* WD19 ...
Elliwood Gdns *GSTN* WD25 ....
Elm Av *OXHEY* WD19 ....
Elmcote Wy *RKW/CH/CXG* WD3 .
Elm Ct *WAT* WD17 * ....
Elm Gv *WATN* WD24 ....
Elmhurst Cl *BUSH* WD23 ....
The Elms *BORE* WD6 * ....
Elm Tree Wk
  RKW/CH/CXG WD3 * ....
Elm Wk *RAD* WD7 ....
Elm Wy *RKW/CH/CXG* WD3 ....
Elmwood Av *BORE* WD6 ....
Elstree Ga *BORE* WD6 * ....
Elstree Hl North *BORE* WD6 ....
Elstree Hl South *BORE* WD6 ....
Elstree Pk *BORE* WD6 * ....
Elstree Rd *BUSH* WD23 ....
Elstree Wy *BORE* WD6 ....
Elton Pk *WAT* WD17 ....
Ely Gdns *BORE* WD6 ....
Embleton Rd *OXHEY* WD19 ....
Empire Centre *WATN* WD24 * ......
Enid Cl *LCOL/BKTW* AL2 ....
Essex La *KGLGY* WD4 ....
Essex Rd *BORE* WD6 ....
  WAT WD17 ....
Estcourt Rd *WAT* WD17 ....
Euston Av *WAT* WD18 ....
Evans Av *GSTN* WD25 ....
Evan's Cl *RKW/CH/CXG* WD3 ......
Evensyde *WATW* WD18 ....
Everett Cl *BUSH* WD23 ....
Exchange Rd *WATW* WD18 ....
Exeter Cl *WATN* WD24 ....
Explorer Dr *WATW* WD18 ....

F

Faggots Cl *RAD* WD7 ....
Fairburn Cl *BORE* WD6 ....
Fair Cl *BUSH* WD23 ....
Fairfield Av *OXHEY* WD19 ....
Fairfield Cl *RAD* WD7 ....
Fairfolds *GSTN* WD25 ....
Fairhaven Crs *OXHEY* WD19 ....
Fairholme Ct *PIN* HA5 * ....
Fairlawns *WAT* WD17 ....
Fairview Dr *WAT* WD17 ....
Fairway Av *BORE* WD6 ....
The Fairway *ABLGY* WD5 ....
Faithfield *BUSH* WD23 * ....
Falconer Rd *BUSH* WD23 ....
Falcon Wy *GSTN* WD25 ....
Falkirk Gdns *OXHEY* WD19 ....
Faraday Cl *WATW* WD18 ....
Farm Cl *BORE* WD6 ....
Farmers Cl *GSTN* WD25 ....
Farm La *RKW/CH/CXG* WD3 ....
Farm Wy *BUSH* WD23 ....
Farraline Rd *WATW* WD18 ....
Farrant Wy *BORE* WD6 ....
Farriers Wy *BORE* WD6 ....
Farthing Cl *WAT* WD17 ....
Fay Gn *ABLGY* WD5 ....
Fearney Md *RKW/CH/CXG* WD3 ..
Fearnley St *WATW* WD18 ....
Featherstone Gdns *BORE* WD6 * ..
Federal Wy *WATN* WD24 ....
Felden Cl *GSTN* WD25 ....
Fell Pth *BORE* WD6 * ....
Felton Cl *BORE* WD6 * ....
Ferndene *LCOL/BKTW* AL2 ....
Ferndown Rd *OXHEY* WD19 ....
Fernhills *KGLGY* WD4 ....
Ferryhills Cl *OXHEY* WD19 ....
Fidler Pl *BUSH* WD23 ....
Field End Cl *OXHEY* WD19 ....
Field Rd *OXHEY* WD19 ....
Field View Ri *LCOL/BKTW* AL2 ....
Field Wy *RKW/CH/CXG* WD3 ....
Fifth Av *GSTN* WD25 ....
Finch Av *RKW/CH/CXG* WD3 ....
Finch La *BUSH* WD23 ....
Finway Ct *WATW* WD18 * ....
Firbank Dr *OXHEY* WD19 ....
First Av *GSTN* WD25 ....
Fir Tree Ct *BORE* WD6 ....

ree HI *RKW/CH/CXG* WD3 ......16 D1
er CI *KGLGY* WD4 ....4 D3
ers CI *BUSH* WD23 ....29 F1
Acres *WATN* WD24 ....9 H4
Acres Av *LCOL/BKTW* AL2 ......7 G3
Fields CI *OXHEY* WD19 ....35 G1
wood Wy *OXHEY* WD19 ....34 D3
nce CI *GSTN* WD25 ....10 B4
tt Dr *ABLGY* WD5 ....9 H5
CI *RAD* WD7 ....13 E5
Pathway *RAD* WD7 ....13 E5
CI *BUSH* WD23 ....30 B1
field *LCOL/BKTW* AL2 ....7 H1
st Rd *GSTN* WD25 ....10 B4
st Wk *BUSH* WD23 ....19 G3
ine La *BORE* WD6 ....32 A3
th Av *GSTN* WD25 ....11 E4
Four Tubs *BUSH* WD23 ....30 C4
BORE WD6 ....32 A3
SH WD23 ....30 A2
ield CI *NTHWD* HA6 ....34 A5
rove Pth *OXHEY* WD19 ....35 E4
ill *WATN* WD24 ....10 B5
ands CI *GSTN* WD25 ....10 A4
ys *OXHEY* WD19 ....35 F2
land Rd *WATW* WD18 ....2 E4
kland CI *RAD* WD7 ....18 D4
kland CI *RKW/CH/CXG* WD3 ....26 D4
kland Rd
W/CH/CXG WD3 ....27 E3
klin Rd *WAT* WD17 ....3 G3
s Wy *WATN* WD24 ....19 C3
La *BORE* WD6 ....4 D4
on CI *OXHEY* WD19 ....34 C1
wood Av *NTHWD* HA6 ....34 A5
isher CI *WATN* WD24 ....29 H3
ord Gv *OXHEY* WD19 ....34 C1
r CI *BUSH* WD23 ....30 C4
rdens *WATN* WD24 ....18 C1
r Rd *WATN* WD24 ....18 C1
r Wy *RKW/CH/CXG* WD3 ....26 D2
nerfield *ABLGY* WD5 ....9 H1
ehill Pde *BORE* WD6 * 32 D1
ehill Rd *BORE* WD6 ....33 E1
e Vw *RKW/CH/CXG* WD3 ....24 B3

G

e CI *ABLGY* WD5 ....9 H1
es Av *BORE* WD6 ....22 C5
lesden Crs *GSTN* WD25 ....11 E3
Av *WD18* 27 H1
e Bank *RKW/CH/CXG* WD3 ......27 G1
CI *WATW* WD18 ....27 H1
Valley *KGLGY* WD4 ....4 D2
View Gdns *KGLGY* WD4 ....9 F1
well CI *GSTN* WD25 ....11 F5
ws HI *KGLGY* WD4 ....5 F5
ws Hill La *ABLGY* WD5 ....5 G5
LGY WD4 ....9 F1
mons Farm CI *WATN* WD24 ....10 A5
mons La *WATN* WD24 ....18 B1
ers Ash *GSTN* WD25 ....10 B2
hill CI *WATN* WD24 ....19 F2
on Wk *OXHEY* WD19 * 35 F3
en CI *WAT* WD17 ....2 A1
en Rd *ABLGY* WD5 ....5 H5
ardens *WAT* WD17 ....18 A4
ield St *WATN* WD24 ....18 C2
en CI *OXHEY* WD19 ....34 C1
ield CI *WAT* WD17 ....2 E3
ett La *LCOL/BKTW* AL2 ....7 G4
ett Dr *LCOL/BKTW* AL2 ....7 G3
atts Rd *BUSH* WD23 ....30 B4
mouth Wy *GSTN* WD25 ....11 E3
con Crs *GSTN* WD25 ....10 D3
con Dr *GSTN* WD25 ....10 D3
con La *GSTN* WD25 ....11 E3
arth *ABLGY* WD5 ....9 G2
et Rd *WAT* WD17 ....3 F2
CI *BORE* WD6 ....23 F3
shead Rd *BORE* WD6 ....22 C4
Gateway *WATW* WD18 ....27 H2
mont Ap *WAT* WD17 * 3 H3
des Rd *BUSH* WD23 * 30 B1
rges Md *BORE* WD6 ....32 B3
rge St *WATW* WD18 ....3 H7
t Tree HI *GSTN* WD25 ....30 C5
ons CI *BORE* WD6 ....22 B3
's Couch *OXHEY* WD19 ....35 E2
t *WATW* WD18 ....27 F3
t's Gn *RKW/CH/CXG* WD3 ......24 C1
HI *RAD* WD7 ....13 G4
Hill La *RAD* WD7 ....13 G4
Hollow *RAD* WD7 ....13 E5
n Rd *BUSH* WD23 ....30 A2
on Wy *BORE* WD6 ....27 F2
rne Wy *WATN* WD24 ....18 B1
stone Rd *WAT* WD17 ....3 H3
Glebe *GSTN* WD25 ....10 D2
CI *WD4* 4 D3
coe Rd *BUSH* WD23 ....29 H3
corse Gn *OXHEY* WD19 * 35 E3
eagles CI *OXHEY* WD19 * 35 E4
haven Av *BORE* WD6 ....22 D5
more Gdns *ABLGY* WD5 ....6 B5
Wy *WAT* WD17 ....17 H2
crest Rd *WAT* WD17 ....3 H3
finch Wy *BORE* WD6 ....30 D1
CI *BUSH* WD23 ....3 K2
ville Av *RKW/CH/CXG* WD3 .....27 E3

Goodison CI *BUSH* WD23 ....30 B2
Goodrich CI *CSTN* WD25 ....10 B4
Goodwood Av *WATN* WD24 ....9 H4
Goodyers Av *RAD* WD7 ....13 E2
Goosefields *RKW/CH/CXG* WD3 .25 H3
Goral Md *RKW/CH/CXG* WD3 ....26 A5
Gorle CI *GSTN* WD25 ....10 B2
Gosforth La *OXHEY* WD19 ....34 B2
Gosforth Pth *OXHEY* WD19 ......34 B2
The Gossamers *GSTN* WD25 .....11 H4
Grace CI *BORE* WD6 ....23 G3
Grandfield Av *WAT* WD17 ....18 A3
Grand Union Canal Wk
KGLGY WD4 ....5 E3
RKW/CH/CXG WD3 ....26 B5
RKW/CH/CXG WD3 ....27 B5
WAT WD17 ....9 F5
WAT WD17 ....17 F1
Grange CI *WAT* WD17 ....18 B3
Grange La *GSTN* WD25 ....20 C3
Grange Rd *BORE* WD6 ....32 C2
BUSH WD23 ....29 F2
Grantham Gn *BORE* WD6 ....33 C5
Granville Rd *WATW* WD18 ....3 C5
Grasmere CI *GSTN* WD25 ....10 C1
Grassington CI *LCOL/BKTW* AL2 .7 F4
Graveley Av *BORE* WD6 ....33 F1
The Graylings *ABLGY* WD5 ....9 G2
Great Gv *BUSH* WD23 ....30 A1
Greatham Rd *BUSH* WD23 ....3 K3
Great Pk *KGLGY* WD4 ....4 A4
Great Westwood *KGLGY* WD4 * ..8 A3
Greenbank Rd *WATN* WD24 ......9 G5
Greenbury CI *RKW/CH/CXG* WD3 .14 B5
Greenfield Av *OXHEY* WD19 .....35 F1
Greenhill Crs *WATW* WD18 ......27 H3
Greenhills *RKW/CH/CXG* WD3 ...25 C2
Green La *OXHEY* WD19 ....28 D4
RKW/CH/CXG WD3 ....26 C2
Greenside *BORE* WD6 ....22 D2
Green St *BORE* WD6 ....22 B1
RKW/CH/CXG WD3 ....14 B4
Greensward *BUSH* WD23 ....30 A3
The Green *RKW/CH/CXG* WD3 ...25 C5
Greenways *ABLGY* WD5 ....5 G5
The Greenway
RKW/CH/CXG WD3 ....25 F4
Greenwood Dr *GSTN* WD25 ......10 A3
Gregson CI *BORE* WD6 ....23 F3
Grenfell CI *BORE* WD6 ....23 F3
Greycaine Rd *WATN* WD24 ....19 E1
Griffon Wy *GSTN* WD25 ....10 A3
Grosvenor Av *KGLGY* WD4 ....5 F2
Grosvenor Ct
RKW/CH/CXG WD3 * 27 G2
Grosvenor Rd *BORE* WD6 ....22 D5
NTHWD HA6 ....34 A3
WAT WD17 ....3 H3
Grosvenor Sq *KGLGY* WD4 ....5 F2
Grove Bank *OXHEY* WD19 * 29 E5
Grove Crs *RKW/CH/CXG* WD3 ....29 D1
Grove Hall Rd *BUSH* WD23 ....29 F1
Grove Mill La *RKW/CH/CXG* WD3 .20 A3
Grove PI *GSTN* WD25 * 20 D3
Grove Rd *BORE* WD6 ....29 E3
The Grove *OXHEY* WD19 ....29 E5
The Grove *RAD* WD7 ....13 F3
RKW/CH/CXG WD3 ....29 D1
Grove Wy *RKW/CH/CXG* WD3 ....24 A1
Grovewood CI
RKW/CH/CXG WD3 ....24 A2
Gulland CI *BUSH* WD23 ....30 B2
Gullet Wood Rd *GSTN* WD25 ....10 B4
Gwent CI *GSTN* WD25 ....11 E3
Gypsy La *KGLGY* WD4 ....9 G4

H

Hackney CI *BORE* WD6 ....33 C2
Haddenham Ct *OXHEY* WD19 * ..35 E2
Haddon CI *BORE* WD6 ....28 D4
Haddon Rd *RKW/CH/CXG* WD3 ..24 B2
Hadley CI *BORE* WD6 ....32 C2
Hadley La *WATN* WD24 ....2 A5
Hagden La *WATW* WD18 ....2 B7
Haggerston Rd *BORE* WD6 ....22 B2
Haines Wy *GSTN* WD25 ....10 B3
Halifax CI *GSTN* WD25 ....10 A3
LCOL/BKTW AL2 ....2 A2
Halifax Rd *RKW/CH/CXG* WD3 ...24 B4
Hallam CI *WATN* WD24 ....18 D4
Hall CI *RKW/CH/CXG* WD3 ....25 F5
Hallowes Crs *OXHEY* WD19 ......34 B2
Halsey PI *WATN* WD24 * 18 C2
Halsey Rd *WATW* WD18 ....2 E3
Halter CI *BORE* WD6 ....33 C3
Hamilton CI *LCOL/BKTW* AL2 ....7 H4
Hamilton Rd *KGLGY* WD4 ....9 F1
OXHEY WD19 ....34 C2
Hamilton St *WATW* WD18 ....3 H7
Hamlet CI *LCOL/BKTW* AL2 ......7 G4
Hammer Pde *GSTN* WD25 * 10 B2
Hampden Wy *WAT* WD17 ....9 H5
Hampermill La *OXHEY* WD19 ....28 B5
Hampstead CI *LCOL/BKTW* AL2 ..7 H4
Hampton CI *BORE* WD6 ....33 F2
Hancock Ct *BORE* WD6 ....23 F3
Handsworth CI *OXHEY* WD19 ....34 B2
Hangar Ruding *OXHEY* WD19 ....35 G2

Hanover Gdns *ABLGY* WD5 * 6 A4
Harborne CI *OXHEY* WD19 ....34 D4
Harcourt Rd *BUSH* WD23 ....30 B2
Harding CI *GSTN* WD25 ....10 D2
The Harebreaks *WATN* WD24 ....18 B1
Hare Crs *GSTN* WD25 ....10 B1
Harewood *RKW/CH/CXG* WD3 ...25 H2
Harewood Rd *OXHEY* WD19 ......34 C1
Harford Dr *WAT* WD17 ....17 H2
Harlech Rd *ABLGY* WD5 ....6 B5
The Harlequin *WAT* WD17 ....3 H4
Harriet Walker Wy
RKW/CH/CXG WD3 ....25 E4
Harriet Wy *BUSH* WD23 ....30 C4
Harris Rd *GSTN* WD25 ....10 B4
Harrogate Rd *OXHEY* WD19 .....34 D2
Harrow Wy *GSTN* WD25 ....35 F2
Hartfield Av *BORE* WD6 ....32 D1
Hartfield CI *BORE* WD6 ....32 D2
Hartforde Rd *BORE* WD6 ....22 D4
Harthall La *KGLGY* WD4 ....5 F2
Harts CI *BUSH* WD23 ....19 H4
Hartspring La *BUSH* WD23 ......20 A3
GSTN WD25 ....20 A3
Harvest End *GSTN* WD25 ....11 E5
Harvest Rd *BUSH* WD23 ....30 A1
Harvey Rd *RKW/CH/CXG* WD3 ...26 D3
Harwoods Rd *WATW* WD18 ......2 C4
Hastings Wy *BUSH* WD23 ....29 F1
RKW/CH/CXG WD3 ....27 E1
Hatfield Rd *WATN* WD24 ....18 C3
Hatters La *WATW* WD18 ....27 G3
Havelock Rd *KGLGY* WD4 ....4 C2
Haweswater Dr *GSTN* WD25 .....10 D2
Hawkesley CI *RAD* WD7 ....13 E4
Hawkins CI *BORE* WD6 ....23 F4
Hawthorn CI *ABLGY* WD5 ....10 A1
WAT WD17 ....18 A2
Hawthorne Rd *RAD* WD7 ....13 F5
Hawtrees *RAD* WD7 ....13 E4
Hay CI *BORE* WD6 ....23 F4
Hayden Dell *BUSH* WD23 ....29 G3
Haydon Dell Farm *BUSH* WD23 *..29 C4
Haydon Rd *OXHEY* WD19 ....29 G3
Hatfield CI *BUSH* WD23 ....30 A1
Hayling Rd *OXHEY* WD19 ....34 B2
Haywood Copse
RKW/CH/CXG WD3 ....26 A1
Haywood Dr *RKW/CH/CXG* WD3 .25 E1
Haywood Pk *RKW/CH/CXG* WD3 .25 E2
Hazelbury Av *ABLGY* WD5 ....9 F1
Hazelcroft *PIN* HA5 ....35 H5
Hazel Gv *GSTN* WD25 ....10 C4
Hazel Tree Rd *WATN* WD24 ......18 C1
Hazelwood La *ABLGY* WD5 ....9 G1
Hazelwood Rd
RKW/CH/CXG WD3 ....27 F3
Healey Rd *WATW* WD18 ....18 A3
Heathbourne Rd *BUSH* WD23 ...31 E5
Heathbrae Mnr *WAT* WD17 * 18 A3
Heather CI *ABLGY* WD5 ....10 B1
Heather Ri *BUSH* WD23 ....19 G4
Heathfield CI *OXHEY* WD19 ......28 D4
Heathfield Rd *BUSH* WD23 ......29 F1
Heath Ldg *BUSH* WD23 * 30 C5
Heath Rd *OXHEY* WD19 ....29 E4
The Heath *RAD* WD7 ....13 F2
Heckford CI *WATW* WD18 ....27 F3
Helston PI *ABLGY* WD5 ....10 A1
Hemingford Rd *WAT* WD17 ......9 H5
Hemming Wy *GSTN* WD25 ....10 B3
Hempstead Rd *KGLGY* WD4 ......4 C1
WAT WD17 ....9 G5
WAT WD17 ....2 C1
Henbury Wy *OXHEY* WD19 ......35 E2
Henderson PI *ABLGY* WD5 ....6 A1
Herga Ct *WAT* WD17 ....18 B4
Heritage Wk
RKW/CH/CXG WD3 * 14 D5
Herkomer CI *BUSH* WD23 ....30 A1
Herkomer Rd *BUSH* WD23 ....29 H1
Herne CI *BUSH* WD23 * 30 B5
Herne Rd *BUSH* WD23 ....30 A3
Heronsgate Rd
RKW/CH/CXG WD3 ....24 A2
Heronslea *GSTN* WD25 ....10 D4
Heswell Gn *OXHEY* WD19 * 34 B2
Heyford Rd *RAD* WD7 ....21 E1
Heysham Dr *OXHEY* WD19 ......34 D4
Hibbert Av *WATN* WD24 ....19 E2
The Hideaway *ABLGY* WD5 ......6 A5
High Acres *ABLGY* WD5 ....9 G1
High Canons *BORE* WD6 ....23 F1
High CI *RKW/CH/CXG* WD3 ......25 H2
High Cross *GSTN* WD25 ....20 C1
High Elms La *GSTN* WD25 ....6 C5
Highfield *KGLGY* WD4 ....4 B2
OXHEY WD19 ....35 E2
Highfield Rd *BUSH* WD23 ....29 F2
Highfields *KGLGY* WD4 * 4 B3
RAD WD7 ....13 E4
Highfield Wy
RKW/CH/CXG WD3 ....25 F3
High Firs *RAD* WD7 ....13 F4
High Md *BUSH* WD23 ....30 A4
Highlands Dr *BUSH* WD23 ....28 D5
The Highlands
RKW/CH/CXG WD3 ....25 G4
GSTN WD25 ....10 A3
High Rd *BUSH* WD23 ....30 C5
High St *ABLGY* WD5 ....6 A1

BORE WD6 ....32 A3
BUSH WD23 ....29 H3
KGLGY WD4 ....4 D5
RKW/CH/CXG WD3 ....26 A5
WAT WD17 ....3 F3
High Vw *RKW/CH/CXG* WD3 .....25 F1
WATW WD18 ....28 A3
Highwood Av *BUSH* WD23 ......19 C3
Hilberry CI *BUSH* WD23 * 30 A4
Hilfield La *GSTN* WD23 ....20 A3
Hillcroft Crs *OXHEY* WD19 ....28 C5
Hill Farm Av *GSTN* WD25 ....10 B2
Hillfield La South *BUSH* WD23 ...30 B3
Hillingdon Rd *GSTN* WD25 ....10 B3
Hillpoint *RKW/CH/CXG* WD3 .....25 H2
Hill Ri *RKW/CH/CXG* WD3 ....25 G4
Hillrise Av *WATN* WD24 ....19 E2
Hillsborough Gn
OXHEY WD19 * 34 B2
Hillside Av *BORE* WD6 ....23 F5
Hillside CI *ABLGY* WD5 ....9 H1
Hillside Crs *OXHEY* WD19 ....29 E3
Hillside Rd *BUSH* WD23 ....29 F2
RAD WD7 ....13 G4
RKW/CH/CXG WD3 ....24 B2
Hilltop Rd *KGLGY* WD4 ....5 G1
Hillview CI *PIN* HA5 ....35 G5
Himalayan Wy *WATW* WD18 ....28 A3
Hindhead Gn *OXHEY* WD19 .....34 D4
Hodges Wy *WATW* WD18 ....28 B3
The Hoe *OXHEY* WD19 ....35 E1
Hogg La *BORE* WD6 ....31 F1
Holbrook Gdns *GSTN* WD25 .....12 A5
Holland Gdns *GSTN* WD25 ....10 D4
Holloway La *RKW/CH/CXG* WD3 .14 A2
Hollybush CI *OXHEY* WD19 ......28 D4
Hollygrove *BUSH* WD23 ....30 C4
Holmdale CI *BORE* WD6 ....22 C4
Holme Lea *GSTN* WD25 ....10 D3
Holme Pk *BORE* WD6 ....22 C4
Holm Oak Pk *WATW* WD18 * 2 C7
Holmside Ri *OXHEY* WD19 ....34 C2
Holt CI *BORE* WD6 ....32 C1
Holtsmere CI *GSTN* WD25 ....10 D4
Holywell Rd *WATW* WD18 ....2 D7
Homefield Rd *BUSH* WD23 ......29 H2
RAD WD7 ....21 E1
RKW/CH/CXG WD3 ....24 C1
Home Park Mill Link Rd
KGLGY WD4 ....5 E5
Homestead Rd
RKW/CH/CXG WD3 ....26 A4
Home Wy *RKW/CH/CXG* WD3 ...25 E5
Hoopers Ms *BUSH* WD23 ....30 A5
Hope Gn *GSTN* WD25 ....10 B2
Hop Garden Wy *GSTN* WD25 ....6 D5
Hopwood CI *WAT* WD17 ....9 C5
Hornbeam CI *BORE* WD6 ....22 D3
Hornbeams *LCOL/BKTW* AL2 ....7 G4
The Hornets *WATW* WD18 ....2 D5
Horseshoe La *GSTN* WD25 ....10 C1
Howard CI *BUSH* WD23 ....30 D4
WATN WD24 ....18 B1
Howard Dr *BORE* WD6 ....33 C1
Howland Ct *PIN* HA5 * 35 H5
Howton PI *BUSH* WD23 ....30 C5
Hoylake Gdns *OXHEY* WD19 .....35 E1
Hubbards Rd
RKW/CH/CXG WD3 ....24 C2
Hudson CI *WATN* WD24 ....10 A5
Hugo CI *WATW* WD18 ....27 H1
Hunter CI *BORE* WD6 ....33 F2
Huntercombe Gdns
OXHEY WD19 ....34 D4
Hunters Ride *LCOL/BKTW* AL2 ...7 H5
Hunter's La *GSTN* WD25 ....10 A3
Hunton Bridge HI *KGLGY* WD4 ...9 F2
Hurricane Wy *ABLGY* WD5 ....10 B2
Hyburn CI *LCOL/BKTW* AL2 ......7 G4
Hyde La *HHS/BOV* HP3 ....7 F4
Hyde Rd *WAT* WD17 ....2 D2
Hyver HI *BAR* EN5 ....33 G3

I

Ilkley Rd *OXHEY* WD19 ....35 E4
Imperial PI *BORE* WD6 * 23 E5
Imperial Wy *WATN* WD24 ....18 D3
Ivinghoe CI *GSTN* WD25 ....11 E4
Ivinghoe Rd *BUSH* WD23 ....30 C3
RKW/CH/CXG WD3 ....28 A1
Ivy Lea *RKW/CH/CXG* WD3 * 25 F5

J

Jacketts Fld *ABLGY* WD5 ....6 A5
James CI *BUSH* WD23 ....29 F2
James Wy *OXHEY* WD19 ....35 E4
Jellicoe Rd *WATW* WD18 ....28 B3
Jenkins Av *LCOL/BKTW* AL2 .....7 F4
Jordan CI *GSTN* WD25 ....10 A4
Jordans Rd *RKW/CH/CXG* WD3 ..25 F4
Jordan's Wy *LCOL/BKTW* AL2 ....7 F4
Jubilee Rd *WATN* WD24 ....18 B2
Judge St *WATN* WD24 ....18 B2
Juniper Av *LCOL/BKTW* AL2 .....7 H5
Juniper Gv *WAT* WD17 ....18 B2

K

Katherine Pl *ABLGY* WD5 ....10 B1
Keble Ter *ABLGY* WD5 ....10 A1
Keele Cl *WATN* WD24.................3 G1
Kelly Cl *BORE* WD6 ....23 G4
Kelmscott Cl *WATM* WD18 ....28 B3
Kelmscott Crs *WATW* WD18..........2 C7
Kelshall *GSTN* WD25 ....11 F5
Kemp Pl *BUSH* WD23 ....29 H3
Kemprow *GSTN* WD25 ....12 C4
Kendals Cl *RAD* WD7 ....12 D5
Kenford Cl *WATN* WD24 ....10 C1
Kenilworth Ct *WAT* WD17 ....18 B3
Kenilworth Dr *BORE* WD6............23 F5
  RKW/CH/CXG WD3................27 E1
Kenilworth Gdns *OXHEY* WD19......34 D4
Kennedy Cl *PIN* HA5..................5 G5
Kensington Av *WATW* WD18 ....2 B5
Kensington Wy *BORE* WD6 ....23 G5
Kent Cl *BORE* WD6 ....23 G2
Keston Ms *WAT* WD17 ....18 C4
Kestrel *GSTN* WD25 ....11 F3
The Kestrels *LCOL/BKTW* AL2 ....7 F5
Kilby Cl *WATN* WD24 ....11 E4
Kilmarnock Rd *OXHEY* WD19 ....35 E3
Kimble Cl *WATW* WD18 * 27 H3
Kimble Crs *BUSH* WD23 ....30 B4
Kimbolton Gn *BORE* WD6............33 F1
Kimpton Pl *GSTN* WD25 ....11 E3
Kindersley Wy *ABLGY* WD5...........5 F5
King Edward Rd *OXHEY* WD19........29 F3
Kingfisher Lure *KGLGY* WD4 * 5 E3
  RKW/CH/CXG 25 G1
King George Av *BUSH* WD23..........30 A3
King Georges Av *WATW* WD18.......2 A5
Kings Av *WATW* WD18 ....2 B5
Kings Cl *NTHWD* HA6.................34 A5
  WATW WD18......................3 G5
Kings Farm Rd
  RKW/CH/CXG WD3................24 C3
Kingsfield Ct *OXHEY* WD19 ....29 E3
Kingsfield Rd *OXHEY* WD19...........29 E4
Kingsley Av *BORE* WD6...............22 C4
Kings Meadow *KGLGY* WD4...........4 D3
King St *WATW* WD18..................3 G5
Kingsway North Orbital Rd
  GSTN 10 B3
Kingswood Rd *BUSH* WD23..........10 C3
Kings Yd *RKW/CH/CXG* WD3 * 26 B5
The Kinnetic Centre
  BORE WD6 *.....................22 D5
Kirby Cl *NTHWD* HA6.................34 A4
Kirkcaldy Gn *OXHEY* WD19...........34 D2
Kitswell Wy *RAD* WD7................13 E2
Knebworth Pth *BORE* WD6...........33 G1
Knowl Wy *BORE* WD6.................32 B2
Knutsford Av *WATN* WD24............19 E2
Koh-i-Noor Av *BUSH* WD23...........29 H3
Kytes Dr *GSTN* WD25 ....11 E2

L

Lady Meadow *KGLGY* WD4 ....4 A1
Ladywood Cl *RKW/CH/CXG* WD3...15 G5
Lady's Cl *WATW* WD18................3 F5
The Lake *BUSH* WD23 ....30 C5
Lake Vw *KGLGY* WD4 * 5 E2
Lamb Cl *GSTN* WD25..................10 D3
Lambert Ct *BUSH* WD23 ....3 K5
Lambourn Cha *RAD* WD7 ....12 D3
Lammas Rd *WATW* WD18.............3 G7
Lamorna Cl *RAD* WD7.................13 G3
Lancaster Wy *ABLGY* WD5............6 A5
Lancing Wy *RKW/CH/CXG* WD3.....27 E2
Lands' End *BORE* WD6................32 A3
Lane Gdns *BUSH* WD23 ....30 D5
Langdale Ter *BORE* WD6 * 23 G5
Langholme *BUSH* WD23 ....30 B5
Langleybury La *KGLGY* WD4 ....9 E3
  RKW/CH/CXG 17 E1
Langley Crs *KGLGY* WD4..............4 D4
Langley Hl *KGLGY* WD4...............4 C3
Langley Hill Cl *KGLGY* WD4...........4 D3
Langley La *ABLGY* WD5...............6 A5
Langley Lodge La *KGLGY* WD4 ......4 B5
Langley Rd *ABLGY* WD5...............5 H5
  WAT WD17 ....18 A3
Langley Wy *WAT* WD17 ....18 A3
Langmead Dr *BUSH* WD23............30 C5
Lapwing Pl *GSTN* WD25 * 10 D1
Lapwing Wy *ABLGY* WD5.............6 B5
Larch Av *LCOL/BKTW* AL2.............7 F4
The Larches *BUSH* WD23..............3 K7
Larken Cl *BUSH* WD23 ....30 B5
Larken Dr *BUSH* WD23 ....30 B5
Latimer Cl *WATW* WD18..............27 H4
Latimer Rd *RKW/CH/CXG* WD3......14 A1
Lauderdale Rd *KGLGY* WD4...........9 F2
Launceston *RKW/CH/CXG* WD3......24 A4
Laurel Cl *OXHEY* WD19 ....29 E4
The Laurels *BORE* WD6 * 22 D4
Lavinia Av *GSTN* WD25 ....10 D3
Lavrock La *RKW/CH/CXG* WD3......26 C4
Lawford Av *RKW/CH/CXG* WD3.....24 B3

Lawford Cl *RKW/CH/CXG* WD3......24 B3
Lawrence Ct *OXHEY* WD19 ....35 E2
Lea Bushes *GSTN* WD25 ....11 F4
Lea Cl *BUSH* WD23....................30 A2
Leaford Crs *WATN* WD24 ....18 A1
Leander Gdns *GSTN* WD25 * 19 F1
Lea Rd *WATN* WD24 * 18 C2
The Leas *BUSH* WD23 ....19 G4
Leavesden Rd *WATN* WD24...........18 C2
Lebanon Rd *WAT* WD17...............9 G5
Le Corte Cl *KGLGY* WD4 ....4 C3
Leeming Rd *BORE* WD6...............22 C3
The Lee *NTHWD* HA6.................34 A4
Leggatts Cl *WATN* WD24..............10 A5
Leggatts Ri *GSTN* WD25 ....10 B4
Leggatts Wy *WATN* WD24.............10 B5
Leggatts Wood Av *WATN* WD24.....10 C5
Leigh Ct *BORE* WD6 * 23 G4
Leigh Rodd *OXHEY* WD19.............35 F2
Lemon Field Dr *GSTN* WD25..........11 F2
Lemonfield Dr *GSTN* WD25...........11 F1
Lemsford Cl *GSTN* WD25..............33 F1
Letchmore Rd *RAD* WD7.............13 F5
Letchworth Cl *OXHEY* WD19.........35 E4
Leven Cl *OXHEY* WD19 * 35 E4
Leveret Cl *GSTN* WD25................10 B5
Lewes Wy *RKW/CH/CXG* WD3......27 E1
Lexington Cl *BORE* WD6 ....22 C5
The Leys *RAD* WD7....................21 F1
Lime Cl *OXHEY* WD19 ....29 E4
The Limes *RKW/CH/CXG* WD3 * 25 H5
Lime Tree Wk *BUSH* WD23...........30 D5
  RKW/CH/CXG 25 G2
Lincoln Ct *BORE* WD6.................33 G2
Lincoln Dr *OXHEY* WD19..............34 D2
  RKW/CH/CXG WD3...............27 E1
Lincoln Wy *RKW/CH/CXG* WD3.....27 E1
Linden Av *WATW* WD18..............2 A4
Linden Lea *GSTN* WD25...............10 B2
Lindiswara Ct
  RKW/CH/CXG WD3...............26 D3
Lingfield Wy *WAT* WD17..............18 A2
Lingmoor Dr *GSTN* WD25.............10 D2
Link Rd *WATN* WD24..................3 J1
Links Dr *BORE* WD6...................22 C5
  RAD WD7.........................13 E2
Links Wy *RKW/CH/CXG* WD3........17 F5
Linnet Cl *BUSH* WD23.................30 B5
Linnet Rd *ABLGY* WD5................6 B5
Linster Gv *BORE* WD6.................33 F2
Linton Av *BORE* WD6..................22 C4
Lion Ct *BORE* WD6....................23 F3
Liphook Rd *OXHEY* WD19.............35 E3
Little Bushey La *BUSH* WD23.........19 H5
  BUSH WD23 ....30 B2
Little Green La
  RKW/CH/CXG WD3...............16 C5
Little Gv *BUSH* WD23 ....30 A1
Little Hayes *KGLGY* WD4..............4 D3
Little Hl *RKW/CH/CXG* WD3..........24 B3
Little How Cft *ABLGY* WD5...........5 F5
Little Martins *BUSH* WD23...........30 A2
Little Orchard Cl *ABLGY* WD5........5 G5
Little Oxhey La *OXHEY* WD19........35 F4
Little Potters *BUSH* WD23............30 D3
Liverpool Rd *WATW* WD18...........3 F6
Loates La *WAT* WD17 ....3 G3
Local Board Rd *WAT* WD17...........3 J6
Lodge Av *BORE* WD6 ....32 C2
Lodge Dr *RKW/CH/CXG* WD3........25 H1
Lodge End *RAD* WD7..................13 G3
  RKW/CH/CXG WD3...............27 G1
Lodge Rd *RKW/CH/CXG* WD3........27 G1
Lombardy Wy *BORE* WD6.............22 B3
London Loop *BORE* WD6.............33 E3
London Rd *BUSH* WD23...............29 H3
Long Barn Cl *GSTN* WD25.............10 B1
Longcliffe Pth *OXHEY* WD19.........34 B2
Long Cft *OXHEY* WD19 ....28 C4
Long Elms *ABLGY* WD5................9 G2
Long Elms Cl *ABLGY* WD5.............9 G2
Long Fallow *LCOL/BKTW* AL2 ....7 H1
Long La *RKW/CH/CXG* WD3..........24 B3
Longmans Cl *WATW* WD18...........27 F3
Longridge *RAD* WD7..................13 G3
Longspring *WATN* WD24..............18 C1
Loom La *RAD* WD7....................13 F5
  RAD WD7.........................21 E1
Lord St *WAT* WD17....................3 G3
Loudwater Dr
  RKW/CH/CXG WD3...............25 H1
Loudwater Hts
  RKW/CH/CXG WD3...............15 G5
Loudwater La
  RKW/CH/CXG WD3...............25 H2
Loudwater Rdg
  RKW/CH/CXG WD3...............25 H1
Louvain Wy *GSTN* WD25..............10 C1
Lovatts *RKW/CH/CXG* WD3...........26 D1
Love La *ABLGY* WD5...................6 A4
  KGLGY WD4 ....4 B3
Lower Derby Rd *WAT* WD17..........3 H5
Lower High St *WAT* WD17............3 H5
Lower Paddock Rd
  OXHEY WD19.....................29 F3
Lower Plantation
  RKW/CH/CXG WD3...............15 H5
Lower Rd *RKW/CH/CXG* WD3........24 C1
Lower Tail *OXHEY* WD19..............35 F2
Lower Tub *BUSH* WD23 ....30 C4

Lowestoft Rd *WATN* WD24...........18 C3
Loweswater Cl *GSTN* WD25...........10 D2
Lowson Gv *OXHEY* WD19.............29 F4
Lowther Cl *BORE* WD6................32 C2
Ludlow Md *OXHEY* WD19.............34 C2
Ludlow Wy *RKW/CH/CXG* WD3......27 E1
Lullington Garth *BORE* WD6 * 33 F2
Lundin Wk *OXHEY* WD19 * 35 E3
Lych Ga *GSTN* WD25 ....11 E2
Lye La *LCOL/BKTW* AL2...............7 H2
Lymington Ct *OXHEY* WD25 * 10 B3
Lyndon Av *PIN* HA5...................35 F5
Lynwood Hts *RKW/CH/CXG* WD3...25 G2
Lysander Wy *ABLGY* WD5.............10 B1
Lytham Av *OXHEY* WD19..............35 E4

M

Mabbutt Cl *LCOL/BKTW* AL2..........7 F4
Macdonnell Gdns *GSTN* WD25.......10 A4
Magnaville Rd *BUSH* WD23...........30 D4
Magnolia Av *ABLGY* WD5.............10 A1
Magpie Pl *GSTN* WD25 ....10 D1
Maiden Flds *BUSH* WD23 ....3 K5
Malden Rd *BORE* WD6................22 D5
  WAT WD17.......................27 H1
Malkin Wy *WATW* WD18.............27 H1
Mallard Rd *ABLGY* WD5...............6 B5
Mallards Ct *OXHEY* WD19............35 G2
Mallard Wy *GSTN* WD25..............11 F5
The Maltings *KGLGY* WD4.............9 F2
Malvern Cl *BUSH* WD23...............30 B3
Malvern Wy *RKW/CH/CXG* WD3....27 E2
Mandela Pl *WATN* WD24.............3 J1
Mandeville Cl *WAT* WD17............18 A2
Manor Ct *RAD* WD7...................21 E1
Manor Dr *LCOL/BKTW* AL2 * 7 H1
Manor House Gdns *ABLGY* WD5.....5 G5
Manor Pl *WATN* WD24................23 E5
Manor Rd *WAT* WD17.................18 C3
Manor Wy *BORE* WD6.................23 F5
  RKW/CH/CXG WD3...............26 D1
Maple Cl *BUSH* WD23.................19 F4
Maple Gv *WAT* WD17.................18 C5
Maple Leaf Cl *ABLGY* WD5...........10 B1
Margaret Cl *ABLGY* WD5..............10 A1
Margeholes *OXHEY* WD19............35 F1
Marian Gdns *GSTN* WD25.............10 C2
Marion Cl *BUSH* WD23................19 G3
Markeston Gn *OXHEY* WD19.........35 E3
Market Pl *WAT* WD17.................3 G4
Market St *WATW* WD18...............3 G4
Markham Rd *BORE* WD6..............22 C5
Marlborough Rd *WATW* WD18.......3 G7
Marlins Cl *RKW/CH/CXG* WD3.......14 D4
Marlins Meadow *WATW* WD18......27 G3
Marlin Sq *ABLGY* WD5................6 A5
The Marlins *NTHWD* HA6.............34 A5
Marriott Ter *RKW/CH/CXG* WD3....25 E1
Marsworth Cl *WATW* WD18 * 27 H3
Martins Cl *RAD* WD7..................12 D5
Marwood Cl *KGLGY* WD4.............4 C3
Maryport Rd *OXHEY* WD19...........34 D3
Masefield Av *BORE* WD6..............33 E2
Mason Cl *BORE* WD6..................23 G3
Matlock Crs *OXHEY* WD19............34 D2
Maude Crs *WATN* WD24...............18 C1
Maxwell Ri *OXHEY* WD19.............29 F4
Maxwell Rd *BORE* WD6...............23 E5
Maycock Gv *NTHWD* HA6............34 A5
Maydwell Ldg *BORE* WD6............22 C5
Mayfare *RKW/CH/CXG* WD3.........27 G2
May Gdns *BORE* WD6.................32 A2
Maylands Rd *OXHEY* WD19...........34 D3
Maythorne Cl *WATW* WD18..........27 G3
Maytree Crs *WATN* WD24............10 A5
Maytrees *RAD* WD7...................21 E1
Meadowbank *KGLGY* WD4...........4 D4
  OXHEY WD19.....................28 D4
Meadow Cl *LCOL/BKTW* AL2 * 7 H1
Meadowcroft *BUSH* WD23 * 30 A3
Meadow Rd *BORE* WD6...............23 E4
  BUSH WD23 ....30 A2
  GSTN WD25 ....10 B3
Meadowside *GSTN* WD25.............10 A5
Meadow Wy *ABLGY* WD5.............6 A1
  KGLGY WD4 ....4 D4
Mead Pl *RKW/CH/CXG* WD3.........25 G5
The Meads *LCOL/BKTW* AL2..........7 H1
The Mead *WATW* WD18..............35 F2
Mead Wy *BUSH* WD23 ....19 H4
Medow Md *RAD* WD7.................13 E2
Medway Cl *WATN* WD25..............10 B5
Meeting Aly *WAT* WD17 * 3 G4
Melbourne Rd *BUSH* WD23...........30 A2
Melia Cl *GSTN* WD25 ....10 D3
Melrose Av *BORE* WD6................33 E4
Melrose Pl *WAT* WD17................18 A2
Mendip Rd *BUSH* WD23...............30 B3
Meriden Wy *GSTN* WD25.............19 F1
Merlin Wy *GSTN* WD25................10 A5
Merry Hill Mt *BUSH* WD23...........30 A5
Merry Hill Rd *BUSH* WD23............29 H4
Merton Rd *WATW* WD18..............2 E5
Meryfield Cl *BORE* WD6...............22 C4
The Metro Centre
  WATW WD18 * 27 F4

Metropolitan Ms *WATW* WD18......2
Metropolitan Station Ap
  WATW WD18......................2
The Mews *WATW* WD18 * 2
Micklefield Wy *BORE* WD6...........2
Middle Down *GSTN* WD25............2
Middle Furlong *BUSH* WD23.........2
Middle Ope *WATW* WD18.............2
Middleton Rd
  RKW/CH/CXG WD3...............2
Middle Wy *WATN* WD24..............2
Mildred Av *BORE* WD6................2
  WATW WD18......................2
Milland Ct *BORE* WD6.................2
Millbrook Rd *BUSH* WD23.............2
Millennium Whf
  RKW/CH/CXG WD3 * 2
Millhouse La *ABLGY* WD5.............2
Mill La *KGLGY* WD4....................2
Millthorne Cl *RKW/CH/CXG* WD3...2
Mill Wy *BUSH* WD23 2
  RKW/CH/CXG WD3...............2
Milner Cl *GSTN* WD25.................2
Milner Ct *BUSH* WD23.................2
Milton Dr *BORE* WD6.................2
Milton St *WATN* WD24................2
Minerva Dr *WAT* WD17...............2
Mitchell Cl *ABLGY* WD5...............2
Moat Cl *BUSH* WD23 2
Moatfield Rd *BUSH* WD23 2
Molteno Rd *WAT* WD17...............2
Moneyhill Ct
  RKW/CH/CXG WD3 * 2
Money Hill Rd *RKW/CH/CXG* WD3...2
Monica Cl *WATN* WD24...............2
Monksmead *BORE* WD6...............2
Monkswood Gdns *BORE* WD6 2
Monmouth Rd *WAT* WD17...........2
Montacute Rd *BUSH* WD23...........2
Montague Hall Pl *BUSH* WD23.......2
Moor Ln *WATW* WD18................2
Moor Lane Crossing
  WATW WD18......................2
Moortown Rd *OXHEY* WD19.........2
Moor Vw *WATW* WD18...............2
Moran Cl *LCOL/BKTW* AL2............2
Morgan Cl *NTHWD* HA6..............2
Morgan Gdns *OXHEY* WD19.........2
Mornington Rd *RAD* WD7............2
Morpeth Av *BORE* WD6...............2
Morriston Cl *OXHEY* WD19...........2
Mortimer Cl *BUSH* WD23.............2
Moss Rd *GSTN* WD25..................2
Moss Side *LCOL/BKTW* AL2...........2
Mostyn Rd *BUSH* WD23...............2
Mount Pleasant La
  LCOL/BKTW AL2 2
The Mount *RKW/CH/CXG* WD3 * 2
Mountview *NTHWD* HA6..............2
Mount Vw *RKW/CH/CXG* WD3.......2
Muirfield Cl *OXHEY* WD19 * 2
Muirfield Gn *OXHEY* WD19...........2
Muirfield Rd *OXHEY* WD19............2
Mulberry Cl *WAT* WD17...............2
Mullion Wk *OXHEY* WD19............2
Munden Gv *WATN* WD24.............2
Mundesley Cl *OXHEY* WD19..........2
Munro Rd *BUSH* WD23................2
Muriel Av *WATW* WD18...............2
Mussenden Ct *WATN* WD24 * 2
Mutchetts Cl *GSTN* WD25.............2

N

Nairn Gn *OXHEY* WD19...............3
Nancy Downs *OXHEY* WD19..........3
Napier Dr *BUSH* WD23................3
The Nap *KGLGY* WD4..................2
Nascot Pl *WAT* WD17.................2
Nascot Rd *WAT* WD17................2
Nascot Wood Rd *WAT* WD17.........2
Nash Cl *BORE* WD6....................2
Neagle Cl *BORE* WD6..................2
Neal St *WATW* WD18..................2
Neild Wy *RKW/CH/CXG* WD3........2
Neptune Ct *BORE* WD6 * 2
Neston Rd *WATN* WD24...............2
Nevill Gv *WATN* WD24................2
Newark Gn *BORE* WD6................2
Newberries Av *RAD* WD7.............2
Newbiggin Pth *OXHEY* WD19........2
Newhouse Crs *GSTN* WD25...........2
Newland Cl *PIN* HA5..................2
Newlands Av *RAD* WD7...............2
Newlands Wk *GSTN* WD25............1
Newlyn Cl *LCOL/BKTW* AL2...........2
New Pde *RKW/CH/CXG* WD3 * 2
Newport Md *OXHEY* WD19 * 2
Newquay Gdns *OXHEY* WD19........2
New Rd *BORE* WD6....................2
  GSTN WD25 1
  RAD WD7.........................2
  RKW/CH/CXG WD3...............2
  RKW/CH/CXG WD3...............2
New St *WAT* WD17....................2
Newton Crs *BORE* WD6................2
Nicholas Cl *WATN* WD24..............2
Nicholas Rd *BORE* WD6...............2

lson Dr *BUSH* WD23 .... 30 B5
 Wy *RKW/CH/CXG* WD3 .... 33 G2
ingale Cl *ABLGY* WD5 .... 6 B5
O WD7 .... 13 E5
ingale Pl
 W/CH/CXG WD3 .... 26 A4
ingale Rd *BUSH* WD23 .... 29 H2
 .... 25 H4
o Dr *BUSH* WD23 .... 30 C4
 Cl *BORE* WD6 .... 23 F3
Side *LCOL/BKTW* AL2 .... 7 H4
ury Av *WATN* WD24 .... 18 D3
k Av *WATN* WD24 .... 18 D3
lk Gdns *BORE* WD6 .... 33 G1
lk House
 W/CH/CXG WD3 * 26 B5
nsfield Cl *BUSH* WD23 .... 30 A4
1 Ap *GSTN* WD25 .... 19 G2
court *RKW/CH/CXG* WD3 * ... 25 F5
field Gdns *WATN* WD24 .... 18 D1
field Rd *BORE* WD6 .... 23 E3
gate Pth *BORE* WD6 .... 26 D2
1 HI *RKW/CH/CXG* WD3 .... 14 D4
1 Orbital Rd
 OL/BKTW AL2 .... 7 F3
1 Orbital Rd St Albans Rd
 TN WD25 .... 7 E5
1 Riding *LCOL/BKTW* AL2 ..... 7 H4
1 Rd *RKW/CH/CXG* WD3 * 26 A5
way *RKW/CH/CXG* WD3 ...... 26 A4
n Western Av *GSTN* WD25 ... 10 A4
 TN WD24 .... 10 A4
n Western Av Coln
 .... 10 D5
n Western Av Gade Side
 LGY WD3 .... 9 F4
n Orbital Av
erspool Wy
 TN WD25 .... 19 G2
wick Rd *OXHEY* WD19 .... 34 D3
n Cl *BORE* WD6 .... 22 D2
rich Wy *RKW/CH/CXG* WD3 .. 17 E5
ngham Cl *GSTN* WD25 .... 10 D3
ngham Rd
 W/CH/CXG WD3 .... 24 B5
llo Wy *BORE* WD6 .... 23 G3
bers Farm *KGLGY* WD4 * 5 F3
ery Cl *OXHEY* WD19 .... 28 C5
ield Cl *RKW/CH/CXG* WD3 * .. 27 E3

O

Av *LCOL/BKTW* AL2 .... 7 H4
ale Cl *OXHEY* WD19 .... 34 D3
ale Rd *OXHEY* WD19 .... 34 D2
ene Rd *WATN* WD24 .... 10 C5
Farm *BORE* WD6 .... 33 F2
 W/CH/CXG WD3 .... 25 F5
ield Cl *BORE* WD6 * 33 E1
 ABLGY WD5 .... 9 H1
hurst Pl *WATW* WD18 * 2 A5
ands Av *OXHEY* WD19 .... 28 C5
ands Ct *WAT* WD17 .... 18 B3
ands Dr *RKW/CH/CXG* WD3 .. 27 F3
eigh Rd *PIN* HA5 .... 35 G5
eade *PIN* WD25 .... 35 H5
dge *LCOL/BKTW* AL2 .... 7 H4
dge Av *RAD* WD7 .... 13 E2
dge La *GSTN* WD25 .... 13 E4
 Cl *RAD* WD7 .... 13 E4
aks *BORE* WD6 * 28 D5
 HEY WD19 .... 28 D5
ree *LCOL/BKTW* AL2 .... 9 G1
ree Ct *BORE* WD6 * 32 A3
iew *WATW* WD18 .... 14 H5
iew Cl *OXHEY* WD19 .... 28 D3
way Pl *RAD* WD7 .... 13 F3
vood Av *WD6* 33 E1
vood Rd *LCOL/BKTW* AL2 ..... 7 G3
d *WAT* WD17 * 3 G4
rver Dr *WATW* WD18 .... 27 H1
pation Rd *WATN* WD18 .... 2 E6
via Ct *WATN* WD24 .... 3 H1
n Pde *RKW/CH/CXG* WD3 * .. 26 C2
sey Rd *BORE* WD6 .... 23 E3
arn La *RKW/CH/CXG* WD3 ... 26 C2
horleywood Rd
 W/CH/CXG WD3 .... 26 A3
ommon Rd
 W/CH/CXG WD3 .... 24 C1
orge Cl *GSTN* WD25 .... 10 B2
louse La *KGLGY* WD4 .... 8 D4
Mill Rd *KGLGY* WD4 .... 9 H3
hire La *RKW/CH/CXG* WD3 ... 4 A3
hire Lane Circular Wk
 .... 24 B4
olesbridge La
 W/CH/CXG WD3 .... 15 F5
Vatford Rd
 OL/BKTW AL2 .... 7 F4
Ap *WATW* WD18 .... 27 E5
Cl *WATW* WD18 .... 27 E5
ne HI *OXHEY* WD19 .... 34 A4
d Crs *GSTN* WD25 .... 10 A4
ard Av *GSTN* WD25 .... 6 C5
ard Cl *BORE* WD6 .... 32 C1
 WD23 .... 30 C5

RAD WD7 .... 20 D1
 RKW/CH/CXG WD3 .... 14 C5
 WAT WD17 .... 18 A4
 WAT WD17 .... 18 A4
Orchard Dr *RKW/CH/CXG* WD3 .. 14 D5
 WAT WD17 .... 18 A4
The Orchard on The Gn
 RKW/CH/CXG WD3 .... 26 C2
The Orchard *KGLGY* WD4 ...... 4 D3
Orchard Wy *RKW/CH/CXG* WD3 .. 25 E5
Organ Hall Rd *BORE* WD6 ..... 22 B3
Oriole Cl *ABLGY* WD5 .... 6 B5
Orion Wy *NTHWD* HA6 .... 34 A3
Ormskirk Rd *WATN* WD19 .... 35 E3
Orphanage Rd *WAT* WD17 .... 3 C1
Orwell Ct *WATN* WD24 .... 3 J1
Osborne Cl *WATN* WD24 .... 18 D2
Osbourne Av *KGLGY* WD4 ...... 4 C2
The Osiers *RKW/CH/CXG* WD3 .. 27 F2
 WATW WD18 .... 27 F3
Osprey Cl *GSTN* WD25 .... 11 E3
Otley Wy *OXHEY* WD19 .... 34 D2
Otterspool La *GSTN* WD25 ... 19 F2
Otterspool Wy *GSTN* WD25 .. 19 G3
Ottoman Ter *WAT* WD17 .... 3 H1
Otway Gdns *BUSH* WD23 ..... 30 D4
Oulton Wy *OXHEY* WD19 ...... 34 C3
Oundle Av *BUSH* WD23 .... 30 B5
Overstream *RKW/CH/CXG* WD3 .. 25 G1
Owens Wy *RKW/CH/CXG* WD3 .. 26 D2
Oxford St *WATW* WD18 .... 2 E6
Oxhey Av *OXHEY* WD19 .... 29 E4
Oxhey Dr *NTHWD* HA6 .... 34 C3
Oxhey La *OXHEY* WD19 .... 29 E4
 PIN HA5 .... 35 A1
Oxhey Ridge Cl *NTHWD* HA6 .. 34 B4
Oxhey Rd *OXHEY* WD19 .... 28 D4

P

Paddock Cl *OXHEY* WD19 ...... 29 F3
Paddock La *BAR* EN5 .... 33 H1
The Paddocks
 RKW/CH/CXG WD3 .... 25 E1
Palace Cl *KGLGY* WD4 .... 4 C4
Palmer Av *BUSH* WD23 .... 30 A2
Palmers Rd *BORE* WD6 .... 23 F3
Pankhurst Pl *WATN* WD24 .... 3 H2
Pankridge *OXHEY* WD19 * 35 E1
The Pantiles *BUSH* WD23 ..... 30 C5
The Parade *OXHEY* WD19 ..... 35 E2
 WAT WD17 .... 2 E2
Parish Cl *GSTN* WD25 .... 10 D3
Park Av *BUSH* WD23 .... 3 A2
 RAD WD7 .... 13 G2
 RKW/CH/CXG WD3 .... 25 F2
 WATW WD18 .... 2 D1
Park Cl *WATN* WD24 .... 3 K2
Park Crs *BORE* WD6 .... 22 C5
Parker St *WATN* WD24 .... 18 C3
Parkfield *RKW/CH/CXG* WD3 .. 25 E1
Parkgate Rd *WATN* WD24 ..... 18 D1
Parklands *BUSH* WD23 * 30 B3
Park Rd *BORE* WD6 .... 29 H3
 RAD WD7 .... 13 F4
 RKW/CH/CXG WD3 .... 26 B4
 WAT WD17 .... 18 B3
Parkside *HHS/BOV* HP3 * 4 D1
 OXHEY WD19 * 28 D3
Parkside Dr *WAT* WD17 .... 17 H4
Parkside Rd *NTHWD* HA6 ..... 34 A4
Park Ter *GSTN* WD25 .... 11 E2
Park View Rd *PIN* HA5 .... 34 C5
Park Wy *RKW/CH/CXG* WD3 .. 25 H5
Parnell Cl *ABLGY* WD5 .... 9 G1
Parpins *KGLGY* WD4 * 4 B2
Parrotts Cl *RKW/CH/CXG* WD3 .. 25 H4
Parsonage Cl *ABLGY* WD5 ..... 5 H4
Parsonage Rd
 RKW/CH/CXG WD3 .... 26 A4
Partridge Cl *BUSH* WD23 * 30 B5
Pasture Cl *BUSH* WD23 .... 30 B4
The Pastures *WATN* WD19 .... 28 C4
The Pathway *OXHEY* WD19 ... 29 E4
Paynesfield Rd *BUSH* WD23 .. 31 E4
Peace Dr *WAT* WD17 .... 2 D1
Pegmire La *WAT* WD17 .... 20 B3
The Pelhams *GSTN* WD25 .... 11 E4
Penman Cl *LCOL/BKTW* AL2 .. 7 H1
Penn Cl *RKW/CH/CXG* WD3 ... 24 C5
Penne Cl *RAD* WD7 .... 13 F3
Penn Rd *RKW/CH/CXG* WD3 .. 25 E5
Penn Wy *RKW/CH/CXG* WD3 . 24 C5
Penrose Av *OXHEY* WD19 ..... 35 E1
Penscroft Gdns *BORE* WD6 ... 33 G1
Penta Ct *BORE* WD6 * 32 D1
Pentland Rd *BUSH* WD23 ..... 30 B3
Percheron Rd *BORE* WD6 ..... 33 G2
Percy Rd *WATW* WD18 .... 3 H4
Peregrine Cl *WATN* WD25 ..... 11 F3
Perivale Gdns *GSTN* WD25 ... 10 C3
Perry Md *BUSH* WD23 .... 30 D3
Pheasants Wy
 RKW/CH/CXG WD3 .... 25 G4
Phillimore Ct *RAD* WD7 * 12 D5
Phillimore Pl *RAD* WD7 .... 12 C5
Phillipers *GSTN* WD25 .... 11 E5
Phoenix Cl *NTHWD* HA6 ...... 34 A4
Pickets Cl *BUSH* WD23 .... 30 C5

Piggy La *RKW/CH/CXG* WD3 .. 24 A3
Pilgrim Cl *GSTN* WD25 .... 11 E2
Piltdown Rd *OXHEY* WD19 .... 35 E1
Pine Gv *BUSH* WD23 .... 19 F4
 LCOL/BKTW AL2 .... 7 G4
Pinehurst Cl *ABLGY* WD5 ...... 9 H1
The Pines *BORE* WD6 .... 22 C4
Pinewood Cl *BORE* WD6 .... 23 G3
 NTHWD HA6 .... 34 B4
 WAT WD17 .... 18 B3
Pinewood Ldg *BUSH* WD23 * .. 30 C5
Pinfold Rd *BUSH* WD23 .... 19 C4
Pinner HI *PIN* HA5 .... 34 D5
Pinner Rd *OXHEY* WD19 .... 29 E3
Pinto Cl *BORE* WD6 * 33 G3
Pioneer Wy *WATW* WD18 ...... 28 A3
The Pippins *GSTN* WD25 ...... 10 D3
Pomeroy Crs *WATN* WD24 .... 10 C5
Popes La *WATN* WD24 .... 18 C1
Pope's Rd *ABLGY* WD5 .... 5 H5
Poplars Cl *OXHEY* WD19 ...... 10 C1
The Poplars *BORE* WD6 .... 22 D3
Potters La *BORE* WD6 .... 22 D5
Potter Street HI *PIN* HA5 ..... 34 C5
Pound Fld *GSTN* WD25 .... 10 H4
Povis Ct *BUSH* WD23 .... 30 C5
Powis Ct *BORE* WD6 .... 23 G5
Premier Pl *WATW* WD18 .... 2 B6
Prestwick Rd *OXHEY* WD19 .. 35 E1
Prestwood *OXHEY* WD19 ...... 35 F1
Pretoria Rd *WATN* WD18 ...... 18 C3
Primrose Gdns *BUSH* WD23 .. 30 A4
Primrose HI *KGLGY* WD4 .... 5 E2
Primrose La *GSTN* WD25 ...... 20 C2
Princes Av *WATN* WD18 .... 2 B6
Prince St *WAT* WD17 .... 3 H3
Priory Vw *BUSH* WD23 .... 30 D4
Pryor Cl *ABLGY* WD5 .... 10 A1
Purbrock Av *GSTN* WD25 ...... 10 D5
Purcell Cl *BORE* WD6 .... 30 A2
Purlings *BUSH* WD23 .... 30 A2
Pursley Gdns *BORE* WD6 ...... 22 D2
Puttenham Cl *OXHEY* WD19 .. 34 D2
Pyot Pth *BORE* WD6 .... 22 D1

Q

Queen Mary's Av *WATW* WD18 .. 27 H1
Queens Av *WATW* WD18 .... 2 B5
Queens Dr *ABLGY* WD5 .... 10 A1
Queenswood Crs *GSTN* WD25 .. 10 B2
The Queen's Dr
 RKW/CH/CXG WD3 .... 25 E3
Queen's Pl *WAT* WD17 .... 3 H3
Queen's Rd *WAT* WD17 .... 3 G4
 WAT WD17 .... 3 G4
Quickley Brow
 RKW/CH/CXG WD3 * 24 A3
Quickley La *RKW/CH/CXG* WD3 .. 24 B3
Quickley Ri *RKW/CH/CXG* WD3 .. 24 A3
Quickly Brow
 RKW/CH/CXG WD3 .... 24 A3
Quickwood Cl
 RKW/CH/CXG WD3 .... 25 E3

R

Radlett Park Rd *RAD* WD7 ..... 13 G3
Radlett Rd *GSTN* WD25 .... 20 B2
 WAT WD17 .... 3 H2
Radnor Hall *BORE* WD6 * 32 B2
Raglan Gdns *OXHEY* WD19 ... 28 C5
Railway Ter *KGLGY* WD4 .... 4 D1
Rainbow Ct *OXHEY* WD19 ..... 28 D3
Ralston Wy *OXHEY* WD19 ..... 35 E1
Randalls Wk *LCOL/BKTW* AL2 .. 7 G4
Ranskill Rd *BORE* WD6 .... 22 D3
Ransom Cl *OXHEY* WD19 ...... 28 D4
Raphael Dr *WATN* WD24 .... 3 J1
Rasehill Cl *RKW/CH/CXG* WD3 .. 25 G4
Raven Cl *RKW/CH/CXG* WD3 .. 25 H4
Ravenscroft *GSTN* WD25 ...... 11 F4
Ravenswood Pk *NTHWD* HA6 .. 34 B5
Raymond Cl *ABLGY* WD5 .... 9 G1
The Readings
 RKW/CH/CXG WD3 .... 15 G5
Rectory La *RKW/CH/CXG* WD3 .. 29 H3
 KGLGY WD4 .... 4 D1
Rectory Rd *RKW/CH/CXG* WD3 .. 26 A4
Reddings *BUSH* WD23 .... 30 A2
The Reddings *BORE* WD6 ..... 22 C5
Redhall La *RKW/CH/CXG* WD3 .. 16 B3
Redheath Cl *GSTN* WD25 ..... 10 A4
Red Lion Cl *GSTN* WD25 ...... 20 A1
Red Rd *BORE* WD6 .... 22 C5
Redwing Gv *ABLGY* WD5 .... 6 B5
Redwood Cl *OXHEY* WD19 .... 34 D3
Redwood Ri *BORE* WD6 .... 22 D1
Reedham Cl *LCOL/BKTW* AL2 .. 7 H1
Reeds Cres *WAT* WD17 .... 3 F1
Regal Wy *WATN* WD24 .... 18 D4
Regent Cl *KGLGY* WD4 .... 4 C3
Regents Cl *RAD* WD7 .... 13 F3
Regent St *WATN* WD24 .... 18 C2
Rendlesham Av *RAD* WD7 .... 21 E1

Rendlesham Wy
 RKW/CH/CXG WD3 .... 24 B3
Repton Dr *RKW/CH/CXG* WD3 .. 26 D2
Reston Cl *BORE* WD6 .... 22 D2
Retford Cl *BORE* WD6 .... 22 D2
Reynard's Wy *LCOL/BKTW* AL2 .. 7 G3
Rhodes Wy *WATN* WD24 ...... 19 E4
Richards Cl *BUSH* WD23 ...... 30 C4
Richfield Rd *BUSH* WD23 ..... 30 A4
Richmond Cl *BORE* WD6 ...... 33 G2
Richmond Dr *WAT* WD17 ...... 17 H4
Richmond Wy
 RKW/CH/CXG WD3 .... 27 F1
Rickmansworth Rd
 RKW/CH/CXG WD3 .... 14 D5
 WAT WD17 .... 2 E3
 WATW WD18 .... 27 H1
Ridgefield *WAT* WD17 .... 17 H1
Ridgehurst Av *GSTN* WD25 ... 10 A2
Ridge La *WAT* WD17 .... 9 H5
Ridge St *WATN* WD24 .... 18 C2
Ridge Wy *RKW/CH/CXG* WD3 .. 25 G4
The Ridgeway *RAD* WD7 .... 21 E1
 WAT WD17 .... 17 H1
Ripon Wy *BORE* WD6 .... 33 F2
The Rise *BORE* WD6 .... 32 C2
Risingholme Cl *BUSH* WD23 .. 30 A4
Riverside Cl *KGLGY* WD4 .... 5 E3
Riverside Dr
 RKW/CH/CXG WD3 .... 26 A5
Riverside Rd *OXHEY* WD19 ... 28 A5
Roberts Rd *WATW* WD18 .... 3 G6
Robeson Wy *BORE* WD6 ...... 23 F3
Robin Hood Dr *BUSH* WD23 .. 19 G3
Robin Pl *GSTN* WD25 .... 10 C1
Robinson Crs *BUSH* WD23 ... 30 B5
Rochester Dr *GSTN* WD25 .... 10 D4
Rochester Wy
 RKW/CH/CXG WD3 .... 27 E1
Rockcliffe Av *KGLGY* WD4 ...... 5 E4
Rockingham Ga *BUSH* WD23 .. 30 B3
Rodgers Cl *BORE* WD6 .... 32 A3
Roman Gdns *KGLGY* WD4 ...... 5 E4
Roman Rd *BORE* WD6 .... 22 A3
 RAD WD7 .... 13 F4
Roman Wk *RAD* WD7 * 13 G5
Romeland *BORE* WD6 .... 32 A3
Romilly Dr *OXHEY* WD19 ...... 35 F3
Rooks HI *RKW/CH/CXG* WD3 .. 25 H1
Rosary Gdns *BUSH* WD23 .... 30 A5
Roseberry Ct *WAT* WD17 ...... 18 B3
Rosebery Rd *BUSH* WD23 .... 30 A5
Rosebriar Wk *WATN* WD24 .... 10 A5
Rosecroft Dr *WAT* WD17 .... 17 H1
Rosedale Cl *LCOL/BKTW* AL2 .. 7 F3
Rose Gdns *WATW* WD18 .... 2 D7
Rosehill Gdns *ABLGY* WD5 .... 9 F1
Rose Lawn *BUSH* WD23 .... 30 B5
The Rose Wk *RAD* WD7 .... 13 G5
Ross Crs *GSTN* WD25 .... 10 B4
Rossington Av *BORE* WD6 .... 22 B2
Rosslyn Rd *WATW* WD18 ...... 2 E3
Ross Wy *NTHWD* HA6 .... 34 A3
Rossway Dr *BUSH* WD23 ...... 30 B2
Rother Ct *GSTN* WD25 .... 10 D3
Roughwood Cl *WAT* WD17 .... 17 H2
Roundbush La *GSTN* WD25 .. 20 B2
The Roundway *WATW* WD18 .. 28 A3
Roundwood *KGLGY* WD4 .... 4 B1
Rousebarn La
 RKW/CH/CXG WD3 .... 16 C2
Rowan Cl *LCOL/BKTW* AL2 ..... 7 H5
Rowlands Av *PIN* HA5 .... 35 G5
Rowley Cl *OXHEY* WD19 .... 29 E5
Rowley La *BAR* EN5 .... 33 H1
 BORE WD6 .... 23 G3
Royce Gv *GSTN* WD25 .... 10 C3
Royston Gv *PIN* HA5 .... 35 G5
Royston Park Rd *PIN* HA5 .... 35 G5
Rudolph Rd *BUSH* WD23 ...... 29 H3
Rufford Cl *WAT* WD17 .... 18 A3
Rugby Wy *RKW/CH/CXG* WD3 .. 27 E2
Rushmore Ct *WATW* WD18 * .. 27 G3
Rushton Av *GSTN* WD25 ...... 10 D4
Russell Crs *GSTN* WD25 .... 10 A4
Russell La *WAT* WD17 .... 9 G5
Russell Wy *OXHEY* WD19 ..... 28 C4
Rutherford Cl *BORE* WD6 ..... 23 F3
Rutherford Wy *BUSH* WD23 .. 30 C5
Rutland Pl *BUSH* WD23 * 30 C5
The Rutts *BUSH* WD23 .... 30 C5
Ryall Cl *LCOL/BKTW* AL2 .... 7 F3
Ryan Ct *OXHEY* WD19 * 29 F4
Ryan Wy *WATN* WD24 .... 18 D3
Ryder Cl *BUSH* WD23 .... 30 A3

S

Saddlers Cl *BORE* WD6 * 33 G2
 PIN HA5 .... 35 H4
Saddlers Wk *KGLGY* WD4 ...... 4 D3
St Albans Rd *GSTN* WD25 ..... 10 D4
 GSTN WD25 .... 11 E3
 WAT WD17 .... 2 E1
 WATN WD24 .... 10 A3
 WATN WD24 .... 18 C2
St Andrews Ct *WAT* WD17 * ... 18 C3
St Andrews Ter *OXHEY* WD19 * .. 34 D4
St Annes Cl *OXHEY* WD19 ..... 34 D3

St Christophers Ct
  RKW/CH/CXG WD3 * 24 C1
St Francis Cl *OXHEY* WD19.........28 C5
St George's Dr *OXHEY* WD19.......35 F2
St George's Rd *WATN* WD24.......18 C2
St James Rd *WATW* WD18...........3 F6
St John's Rd *WAT* WD17............3 F1
St Lawrence Cl *ABLGY* WD5........5 H4
St Lawrence Wy
  LCOL/BKTW AL2...................7 G4
St Leonards Cl *BUSH* WD23.......29 F1
St Martins Cl *OXHEY* WD19........34 D3
St Marys Cl *WATW* WD18 *.........3 G4
St Marys Ter *BORE* WD6 *.........32 A3
St Marys Vw *WATW* WD18 *........3 G5
St Mary's Rd *WATW* WD18..........3 F5
St Matthews Cl *OXHEY* WD19......29 E3
St Michaels Dr *GSTN* WD25........10 C2
St Neots Cl *BORE* WD6............22 D2
St Nicholas Cl *BORE* WD6.........32 A3
St Pauls Wy *WATN* WD24...........3 H1
St Paul's Cl *BORE* WD6...........33 F2
St Peters Wy *RKW/CH/CXG* WD3 ..24 A1
St Peter's Cl *BUSH* WD23.........30 C5
St Vincents Cottages
  WATW WD18 *.....................3 F4
Salisbury Rd *WATN* WD24..........18 C2
Salters Cl *RKW/CH/CXG* WD3......26 B5
Salters Gdns *WAT* WD17 *.........18 B3
Sandown Rd *WATN* WD24...........18 C2
Sandringham Rd *WATN* WD24......18 C1
Sandy La *BUSH* WD23..............20 B5
  NTHWD HA6.......................34 A1
Sandy Ldg *PIN* HA5 *.............35 H5
Sarratt La *RKW/CH/CXG* WD3.......15 G4
Sarratt Rd *RKW/CH/CXG* WD3.......15 G1
Sawtry Wy *BORE* WD6..............22 D2
Saxon Ct *BORE* WD6...............22 B3
Saxton Ms *WAT* WD17 *............18 B3
Scammell Wy *WATW* WD18..........28 A3
School La *BUSH* WD23.............30 A5
  LCOL/BKTW AL2...................11 G3
School Md *ABLGY* WD5..............9 G1
Schubert Rd *BORE* WD6............32 A3
Scotscraig *RAD* WD7..............13 E4
Scots Hl *RKW/CH/CXG* WD3.........26 C3
Scots Hill Cl *RKW/CH/CXG* WD3....26 C3
Scots Mill La *RKW/CH/CXG* WD3....26 C3
Scottswood Cl *BUSH* WD23.........19 F4
Scottswood Rd *BUSH* WD23.........19 F4
Scrubbits Sq *RAD* WD7............13 F4
Scrubbitts Park Rd *RAD* WD7......13 F4
Seabrook Rd *KGLGY* WD4...........5 G2
Seacroft Gdns *OXHEY* WD19........35 E2
Searches La *ABLGY* WD5............6 D1
Second Av *GSTN* WD25.............11 E4
Sequoia Cl *BUSH* WD23............30 C5
Seven Acres *NTHWD* HA6...........34 B5
Severn Wy *GSTN* WD25.............10 D3
Shackleton Wy *ABLGY* WD5 *.......10 B1
Shady Bush Cl *BUSH* WD23.........30 B4
Shady La *WAT* WD17................3 F1
Shaftesbury Ct
  RKW/CH/CXG WD3.................27 F2
Shaftesbury Rd *WAT* WD17 *.......3 H3
Shaftsbury Wy *KGLGY* WD4.........5 F1
Shakespeare St *WATN* WD24........18 C2
Shanklin Gdns *OXHEY* WD19........34 A4
Sheepcot Dr *GSTN* WD25...........10 D3
Sheepcot La *GSTN* WD25...........10 D3
Shelley Cl *NTHWD* HA6.............34 A4
Shelly Cl *BORE* WD6...............32 D1
Shenley Hl *RAD* WD7...............13 G3
Shenley Rd *BORE* WD6.............32 C2
Shepherd Cl *ABLGY* WD5............6 A4
Shepherds Rd *WATW* WD18..........2 B3
Shepherds Wy
  RKW/CH/CXG WD3.................25 G4
Shepherd's La
  RKW/CH/CXG WD3.................24 C3
Shepperton Cl *BORE* WD6.........23 E3
Sheppey's La *KGLGY* WD4...........5 H2
Sheraton Cl *BORE* WD6............32 C2
Sheraton Ms *WATW* WD18 *.........27 H1
Sherborne Wy
  RKW/CH/CXG WD3.................27 E1
Sheridan Rd *OXHEY* WD19..........29 E4
Sheriff Wy *GSTN* WD25............10 B2
Sherland Ct *RAD* WD7 *...........13 F4
Sherwoods Rd *OXHEY* WD19.........29 F4
Shetland Cl *BORE* WD6............33 G2
Shire La *RKW/CH/CXG* WD3.........24 A2
Shiremeade *BORE* WD6.............32 C2
The Shires *GSTN* WD25.............6 C5
Shirley Rd *ABLGY* WD5............10 A1
Short La *LCOL/BKTW* AL2............7 F3
Sidmouth Cl *OXHEY* WD19..........34 C1
Silk Mill Rd *OXHEY* WD19.........28 C4
Silverdale Rd *BUSH* WD23.........30 B1
Silver Dell *WATN* WD24...........10 A4
Silver Trees *LCOL/BKTW* AL2.......7 G4
Sinderby Cl *BORE* WD6............22 B3
Sirus Rd *NTHWD* HA6..............34 B4
Siskin Cl *BORE* WD6..............32 D1
  BUSH WD23......................29 F1
Sixth Av *GSTN* WD25..............11 E4
Skidmore Wy
  RKW/CH/CXG WD3.................26 B5
Slade Ct *RAD* WD7................13 F4
Sleaford Gn *OXHEY* WD19..........35 E2
Smith St *WATW* WD18...............3 G5

Solar Ct *WATW* WD18 *.............2 A6
Solesbridge Cl
Solesbridge La
  RKW/CH/CXG WD3.................15 E5
Solomon's Hl *RKW/CH/CXG* WD3....26 A4
Somers Wy *BUSH* WD23.............30 B4
Sonia Cl *OXHEY* WD19.............28 D4
Sotheron Rd *WAT* WD17.............3 H1
Souldern St *WATW* WD18............2 D1
South Cottage Dr
  RKW/CH/CXG WD3.................25 E2
South Cottage Gdns
  RKW/CH/CXG WD3.................25 E2
Southfield Av *WATN* WD24.........18 D2
South Park Av
  RKW/CH/CXG WD3.................25 E2
South Riding *LCOL/BKTW* AL2......7 H4
South Rd *RKW/CH/CXG* WD3.........24 B2
Southsea Av *WATW* WD18............2 C4
South View Rd *PIN* HA5...........34 C5
South Vw *ABLGY* WD5..............9 H2
  KGLGY WD4.......................9 H2
Southwood Rd *WATN* WD24.........18 D1
Sparrows Herne *BUSH* WD23........30 A4
Sparrows Wy *BUSH* WD23...........30 B5
Sparrows Wick *BUSH* WD23 *.......30 B5
Sparrow Wk *GSTN* WD25............10 B4
Spencer Ms *RKW/CH/CXG* WD3......25 H2
The Spinney *GSTN* WD25...........20 B2
  WAT WD18........................18 B3
Spring Cl *BORE* WD6..............22 D4
Spring Crofts *BUSH* WD23.........29 H2
Springfield *BUSH* WD23...........30 C5
Springfield Cl
  RKW/CH/CXG WD3.................27 E2
Springfield Rd *GSTN* WD25........10 C2
Spring Gdns *GSTN* WD25...........10 D4
Spur Cl *ABLGY* WD5................9 C2
The Square *WATN* WD24............18 C1
The Squirrels *BUSH* WD23.........30 C3
Stag La *RKW/CH/CXG* WD3..........24 B3
Stainer Rd *BORE* WD6.............22 A3
Stamford Rd *WAT* WD17............18 C4
Stanborough Av *BORE* WD6.........22 D2
Stanbury Av *WAT* WD17............17 H1
Standfield *ABLGY* WD5.............5 H5
Stangate Crs *BORE* WD6...........33 H2
Stanley Gdns *BORE* WD6...........22 B3
Stanley Rd *WAT* WD17.............3 H3
Stanmore Rd *WATN* WD24..........18 C3
Stapleton Rd *BORE* WD6...........22 D2
Starling Pl *GSTN* WD25 *.........10 D1
Station Ap *OXHEY* WD19............35 E2
  RAD WD7.........................13 F4
  RKW/CH/CXG WD3.................24 B1
  WATW WD18 *.....................2 A4
Station Footpath *KGLGY* WD4......5 E4
Station Rd *BORE* WD6.............32 D1
  KGLGY WD4.......................5 E3
  LCOL/BKTW AL2...................7 H5
  RAD WD7.........................13 F4
  RKW/CH/CXG WD3.................26 A4
  WAT WD17........................18 C4
Steeplands *BUSH* WD23............30 A4
Stephenson Wy *BUSH* WD23.........19 E3
  WATN WD24.......................3 K3
Stevenage Crs *BORE* WD6..........22 B3
Stevens Gn *BUSH* WD23............30 B5
Stewart Cl *ABLGY* WD5.............6 B5
Stilton Pth *BORE* WD6............22 D2
Stirling Wy *ABLGY* WD5...........10 B1
  BORE WD6........................33 G3
Stockport Rd *RKW/CH/CXG* WD3....24 B4
Strangeways *WAT* WD17.............9 H5
Stratfield Rd *BORE* WD6..........22 C5
Stratford Rd *WAT* WD17...........18 B4
Stratford Wy *LCOL/BKTW* AL2......7 G3
  WAT WD17........................2 B1
Stretton Wy *BORE* WD6............22 B2
Stripling Wy *WATW* WD18..........28 B3
Stuart Ct *BORE* WD6..............32 A3
Stud Gn *GSTN* WD25...............10 D1
The Studios *BUSH* WD23...........29 H3
Studio Wy *BORE* WD6..............23 F3
Suffolk Cl *BORE* WD6.............33 G2
Sullivan Wy *BORE* WD6............31 H3
Summerfeld Rd *GSTN* WD25.........10 B4
Summer Gv *BORE* WD6..............32 A3
Summer Hl *BORE* WD6..............32 D2
Summerhouse La *GSTN* WD25........20 B3
Summerhouse Wy *ABLGY* WD5........6 A4
Summer Pl *WATW* WD18 *...........28 A3
Summers Wd *BORE* WD6 *...........33 E1
Sunderland Gv *GSTN* WD25.........10 A3
Sussex Rd *WATN* WD24.............18 B2
Sutcliffe Cl *BUSH* WD23..........30 B1
Sutton Rd *WAT* WD17..............3 G3
Swallow Cl *BUSH* WD23............30 A5
  RKW/CH/CXG WD3.................25 H4
Swallow Oaks *ABLGY* WD5..........5 H4
Swan Cl *RKW/CH/CXG* WD3..........26 A4
Swanston Pth *OXHEY* WD19.........34 D2
Swiss Av *WATW* WD18..............27 H1
Swiss Cl *WATW* WD18..............17 H5
Sycamore Ap *RKW/CH/CXG* WD3.....19 F4
Sycamore Cl *BUSH* WD23...........10 C4
  GSTN WD25.......................10 C4
Sycamore Rd *RKW/CH/CXG* WD3.....27 F2
The Sycamores *RAD* WD7...........13 G3

Sydney Rd *WATW* WD18.............27 H2
Sylvia Av *PIN* HA5...............35 G5

T

Talbot Av *OXHEY* WD19............29 F4
Talbot Rd *RKW/CH/CXG* WD3........26 B5
Tallis Wy *BORE* WD6..............22 A3
Tanners Hl *ABLGY* WD5.............6 A5
Tanners Wood La *ABLGY* WD5.......9 H1
Tate Gdns *BUSH* WD23.............30 D4
Tauber Cl *BORE* WD6..............32 C1
Tavistock Rd *WATN* WD24..........11 E3
Telford Cl *GSTN* WD25............11 E4
Temple Cl *WAT* WD17..............18 A4
Templepan La
  RKW/CH/CXG WD3.................16 B1
Tempsford Av *BORE* WD6...........33 G1
Tennison Av *BORE* WD6............33 E2
Terrace Gdns *WAT* WD17...........18 C4
Thellusson Wy
  RKW/CH/CXG WD3.................25 E4
Theobald Ct *RAD* WD7 *...........13 F4
Theobald St *BORE* WD6............22 A2
Third Av *GSTN* WD25..............11 E6
Thirsk Rd *BORE* WD6..............22 D2
Thompson Wy
  RKW/CH/CXG WD3.................25 E4
Thorn Av *BUSH* WD23..............30 B5
Thornbury Gdns *BORE* WD6.........33 F1
Thorndyke Ct *PIN* HA5............35 H5
Thornton Gv *PIN* HA5.............35 H5
Thorpe Crs *OXHEY* WD19...........28 C4
Three Valleys Wy *BUSH* WD23.....3 K6
Thrift Farm La *BORE* WD6.........22 B3
Throstle Pl *GSTN* WD25 *.........10 D1
Thrums *WATN* WD24................18 C1
Thrush Gn *RKW/CH/CXG* WD3........25 H4
Tibbles Cl *GSTN* WD25............11 F4
Tibbs Hill Rd *ABLGY* WD5..........6 A4
Tilehouse La *BORE* WD6...........22 C5
Timberidge *RKW/CH/CXG* WD3.......25 E4
Tinwell Ms *BORE* WD6.............33 G2
Tithe Barn Cl *ABLGY* WD5 *.......6 A5
Titian Av *BUSH* WD23.............30 D4
Tollgate Cl *RKW/CH/CXG* WD3......25 E1
Tolpits Cl *WATW* WD18............2 A7
Tolpits La *WATW* WD18............27 G4
Tomkins Cl *BORE* WD6.............22 B3
Tom's La *KGLGY* WD4...............5 F2
Tooveys Mill Cl *KGLGY* WD4.......4 D3
Torworth Rd *BORE* WD6............33 G1
Townfield *RKW/CH/CXG* WD3........26 A4
Trefusis Wk *WAT* WD17............17 H3
Trevallance Wy *GSTN* WD25........10 D2
Trevose Wy *OXHEY* WD19...........34 D2
Trident Rd *GSTN* WD25............10 A3
Trinity Hall Cl *WATN* WD24.......3 H1
Tristan Ldg *BUSH* WD23 *.........29 F1
Trout Ri *RKW/CH/CXG* WD3.........15 G5
Troutstream Wy
  RKW/CH/CXG WD3.................25 G1
Trowley Ri *ABLGY* WD5............5 H5
Trundlers Wy *BUSH* WD23..........30 D5
Tucker St *WATW* WD18.............3 G6
Tudor Av *GSTN* WD25..............11 E1
Tudor Ct *BORE* WD6...............22 B4
Tudor Dr *WATN* WD24..............19 E2
Tudor Manor Gdns *GSTN* WD25.....11 E1
Tudor Wk *WATN* WD24..............19 E1
Tudor Wy *RKW/CH/CXG* WD3.........25 F5
Tunnel Wood Cl *WAT* WD17.........18 A1
Tunnel Wood Rd *WAT* WD17.........18 A1
Turnberry Ct *OXHEY* WD19.........34 D2
Turnberry Dr *LCOL/BKTW* AL2......7 F4
Turner Rd *BUSH* WD23.............30 B1
Turneys Orch *RKW/CH/CXG* WD3....24 C2
The Turnstones *GSTN* WD25........10 D1
Tussauds Cl *RKW/CH/CXG* WD3.....26 D2
Tylers Cl *KGLGY* WD4.............4 C3
Tylersfield *ABLGY* WD5............6 A5

U

University Cl *BUSH* WD23.........29 G1
Uplands *RKW/CH/CXG* WD3..........26 C3
The Uplands *LCOL/BKTW* AL2.......7 F4
Upper Hwy *KGLGY* WD4.............9 F1
Upper Hill Ri *RKW/CH/CXG* WD3....25 E2
Upper Hitch *OXHEY* WD19..........29 F5
Upper Paddock Rd
  OXHEY WD19......................29 F3
Upper Station Rd *RAD* WD7........13 F4
Upper Tail *OXHEY* WD19...........35 E2
Upton Lodge Cl *BUSH* WD23........30 B4
Upton Rd *WATW* WD18..............2 E4
Uxbridge Rd *RKW/CH/CXG* WD3.....25 G5

V

Vale Av *BORE* WD6................33 E2
Valency Cl *NTHWD* HA6............34 A3
Vale Rd *BUSH* WD23...............29 F2
Valley Pk *WATW* WD18 *...........27 F4

Valley Ri *GSTN* WD25
Valley Rd *RKW/CH/CXG* WD3........25 G3
Valley Wk *RKW/CH/CXG* WD3
Vega Crs *NTHWD* HA6
Vega Rd *BUSH* WD23
Venice Av *WATW* WD18
  WATW WD18
Vera Ct *OXHEY* WD19
Ver-colne Valley Wk *GSTN* WD25...
  WAT WD17
Verdure Cl *GSTN* WD25
Vernon Rd *BUSH* WD23
Vicarage La *KGLGY* WD4
Vicarage Rd *WATW* WD4
  WATW WD18
  WATW WD18
Victoria Cl *RKW/CH/CXG* WD3
Victoria Rd *BUSH* WD23
  WATN WD24
Victor Smith Ct
  LCOL/BKTW AL2 *
Villiers Rd *OXHEY* WD19
Violet Wy *RKW/CH/CXG* WD3
Vivian Cl *OXHEY* WD19
Vivian Gdns *OXHEY* WD19

W

Wadham Rd *ABLGY* WD5
Wagon Wy *RKW/CH/CXG* WD3
Walnut Gn *BUSH* WD23
Walpole Cl *PIN* HA5
Walshford Wy *BORE* WD6
Walton Rd *BUSH* WD23
Walverns Cl *WATW* WD18
Wansford Pk *BORE* WD6
Wards La *BORE* WD6
Warenford Wy *BORE* WD6
Warneford Pl *OXHEY* WD19
Warren Gv *BORE* WD6
Warren Rd *BUSH* WD23
The Warren *KGLGY* WD4
  RAD WD7
Warwick Cl *BUSH* WD23
Warwick Ct *RKW/CH/CXG* WD3
Warwick Pl *BORE* WD6 *
Warwick Rd *BORE* WD6
Warwick Wy *RKW/CH/CXG* WD3
Water End Cl *BORE* WD6
Waterfield *RKW/CH/CXG* WD3
Waterfields Wy *BUSH* WD23
The Waterfront *BORE* WD6 *
The Watergate *OXHEY* WD19
Water La *KGLGY* WD4
  WAT WD17
Waterman Cl *OXHEY* WD19
Waters Dr *RKW/CH/CXG* WD3
Waterside *KGLGY* WD4
  RAD WD7
Waterside Ct *KGLGY* WD4
Watford Field Rd *WATW* WD18
Watford Heath *OXHEY* WD19
Watford Heath Farm
  OXHEY WD19 *
Watford Int *WATN* WD24 *
Watford Rd *BORE* WD6
  KGLGY WD4
  KGLGY WD4
  LCOL/BKTW AL2
  NTHWD HA6
  RAD WD7
  RKW/CH/CXG WD3
Watling Knoll *RAD* WD7
Watling St *RAD* WD7
Wayside Av *BUSH* WD23
Weall Gn *GSTN* WD25
Webber Cl *BORE* WD6
Welbeck Cl *BORE* WD6
Welham Cl *BORE* WD6
Well End Rd *BORE* WD6
Wellesley Av *NTHWD* HA6
Wellington Cl *OXHEY* WD19
Wellington Rd *WAT* WD17
Wellsfield *BUSH* WD23
Welstones *WAT* WD17
Wendover Wy *BUSH* WD23
Wensum Wy *RKW/CH/CXG* WD3
Wentbridge Pth *BORE* WD6
Wentworth Av *BORE* WD6
Wentworth Cl *WAT* WD17
Westbury Rd *WATW* WD18
West Dr *GSTN* WD25
Westfield Av *WATN* WD24
Westland Cl *GSTN* WD25
Westland Rd *WAT* WD17
Westlea Av *GSTN* WD25
West Riding *LCOL/BKTW* AL2
West St *WAT* WD17
Westview Ct *BORE* WD6
West View Gdns *BORE* WD6
West Wy *RKW/CH/CXG* WD3
Westwick Pl *GSTN* WD25
Wetherby Rd *BORE* WD6
Wharf La *RKW/CH/CXG* WD3
Wheatley Dr *GSTN* WD25
Wheelright Cl *BUSH* WD23
Whippendell Rd *WATW* WD18
Whisper Wd *RKW/CH/CXG* WD3

Craig Cl *PIN* HA5 ....35 H4
gates Cl
/CH/CXG WD3.................26 D1
house Av *BORE* WD6.........26 D1
lands Av
N/CH/CXG WD3.................14 A5
Shack La
N/CH/CXG WD3.................16 C1
ield Wy *RKW/CH/CXG* WD3...25 E5
rs Dr *KGLGY* WD4...............4 C2
y Cl *ABLGY* WD5................10 B1
le Cl *GSTN* WD25...............10 A3
well Rd *GSTN* WD25.............11 E4
on Wy *GSTN* WD25...............11 E5
nhall Rd *WATW* WD18...........3 F5
n Wy *GSTN* WD25...............11 E3
Av *OXHEY* WD19................29 F4
Cl *OXHEY* WD19................29 F4
x Cl *BORE* WD6.................23 F3
cres *NTHWD* HA6................34 A3
aks Cl *NTHWD* HA6.............34 A3
ood Av *LCOL/BKTW* AL2.......7 G4
son Wy
N/CH/CXG WD3.................25 F5
n St *BUSH* WD23................3 K3
ms Wy *RAD* WD7.................13 D5
Dene *BUSH* WD23...............30 D4
Edge *KGLGY* WD4................4 D3

Willow End *NTHWD* HA6.........34 B5
Willow La *WATW* WD18...........2 D7
The Willows *BORE* WD6 *.......22 B3
    OXHEY WD19.................28 C4
Willow Wy *LCOL/BKTW* AL2......7 H1
    RAD WD7....................12 D5
Wimborne Gv *WAT* WD17.........17 H1
Winchester Wy
    RKW/CH/CXG WD3............27 E2
Winchfield Wy
    RKW/CH/CXG WD3............25 H4
Windermere Cl
    RKW/CH/CXG WD3............24 C2
Windmill Dr *RKW/CH/CXG* WD3...26 C3
Windmill La *BUSH* WD23.........30 D5
Windmill St *BUSH* WD23.........30 D5
Windsor Rd *WATN* WD24.........18 D2
Windsor Wy *RKW/CH/CXG* WD3...25 F5
Wingfield Ct *WATW* WD18 *......27 G3
Winstre Rd *BORE* WD6..........22 D3
Winton Ap *RKW/CH/CXG* WD3....27 F2
Winton Crs *RKW/CH/CXG* WD3...27 F2
Winton Dr *RKW/CH/CXG* WD3....27 F2
The Wintons *BUSH* WD23 *......30 C5
Witney Cl *PIN* HA5.............35 G5
Woburn Cl *BUSH* WD23..........30 B3
Woodbank *RKW/CH/CXG* WD3....25 H3
Woodfield Ri *BUSH* WD23.......30 C4

Woodfield Rd *RAD* WD7.........13 F5
Woodfields *WATW* WD18 *.......3 G5
Woodford Rd *WAT* WD17.........3 G1
Woodgate *GSTN* WD25..........10 C2
Woodgate Crs *NTHWD* HA6......34 B5
Woodgate Ms *WAT* WD17........18 B5
Woodhall La *OXHEY* WD19.......35 E2
Woodhouse Eaves *NTHWD* HA6...34 B4
Woodhurst Av *GSTN* WD25.......11 E4
Woodland Dr *WAT* WD17..........2 C1
Woodland La
    RKW/CH/CXG WD3............14 C5
Woodlands *RAD* WD7............13 F3
Woodlands Cl *BORE* WD6........33 E1
Woodlands Dr *KGLGY* WD4.......5 F2
Woodlands Rd *BUSH* WD23......29 F1
    HHS/BOV HP3.................4 C5
Woodland Wy *ABLGY* WD5........6 A1
Woodmans Yd *WAT* WD17.........3 H5
Woodmere Av *WATN* WD24.......19 E2
Woodpecker Cl *BUSH* WD23......30 B5
Woodshots Meadow
    WATW WD18...................27 G2
Woodside *BORE* WD6............32 C1
    WAT WD17...................18 B1
Woodside Ct *GSTN* WD25........10 D2
Woodside Rd *ABLGY* WD5.........6 C5
    LCOL/BKTW AL2...............7 G4

The Woods *NTHWD* HA6.........34 B4
    RAD WD7....................13 G3
Woodstock Rd *BUSH* WD23......30 D4
Woodville Court Ms
    WAT WD17 *..................18 B4
Woodwaye *OXHEY* WD19.........28 D3
Woolmer Ct *BORE* WD6..........22 D2
Woolmerdine Ct *BUSH* WD23.....3 K3
Wordsworth Gdns *BORE* WD6....32 D2
Wren Crs *BUSH* WD23...........30 B5
Wyatt Cl *BUSH* WD23...........30 D4
Wyatt's Cl *RKW/CH/CXG* WD3...15 F5
Wyatt's Rd *RKW/CH/CXG* WD3...25 E1

Y

Yarmouth Rd *WATN* WD24........18 C2
Ye Cnr *OXHEY* WD19.............29 E3
Yew Tree Ct *BORE* WD6.........32 A3
York Cl *KGLGY* WD4..............4 D3
York Crs *BORE* WD6.............23 G4
Yorke Ga *WAT* WD17............18 B4
Yorke Rd *RKW/CH/CXG* WD3.....26 D3
York Rd *WATW* WD18.............3 H7
York Wy *GSTN* WD25............11 E5
Yule Cl *LCOL/BKTW* AL2.........7 G4

Index - featured places

ts Langley Primary School
    GY WD5......................5 H3
tswood Medical Centre
    GY WD5.....................10 B1
Wood Primary School
    N WD25.....................10 C2
ham Country Park
    RE WD6.....................31 G2
ham Golf & Country Club
    N WD25.....................20 A2
ham Preparatory School
    RE WD6.....................21 E4
t Hills Primary School
    N/CH/CXG WD3...............25 F3
ld Junior School
    H WD23.....................30 A4
edford Arms Hotel
    N/CH/CXG WD3...............14 A2
ond JMI School
    GY WD5......................6 A2
field JMI School
    N WD24.....................18 B1
ley Clinic
    N/CH/CXG WD3...............25 H5
Western White House
    tel
    TW WD18.....................2 E4
amwood FC
    RE WD6.....................23 E4
amwood Industrial Park
    RE WD6.....................23 G4
yard 25 Retail Park
    RE WD6.....................22 D5
hehall J & I School
    H WD23.....................29 H2
kspeare School
    GY WD5......................5 H5
et Primary School
    HEY WD19...................29 E4
ey Golf & Country Club
    H WD23.....................29 H3
ey Hall Golf Club
    H WD23.....................29 G1
ey Hall School
    H WD23.....................29 G3
ey Hall Swimming Pool
    H WD23.....................29 G2
ey Health Centre
    H WD23.....................29 G3
ey Heath Primary School
    H WD23.....................30 C5
ey Manor Junior School
    H WD23.....................29 G2
ey Meads School
    H WD23.....................30 B2
ey Museum & Art Gallery
    H WD23.....................29 H3
et Industrial Estate
    TW WD18....................27 F5
al Business Centre
    TN WD24....................11 E5
f Road Industrial Estate
    W WD18.....................28 C3
nders Park Cemetery
    HEY WD19...................35 G3
bury Junior School
    T WD17.....................17 H3
al Primary School
    T WD17......................3 H4
er Infant School
    ....2 C5
er Junior School
    TW WD18.....................2 D5
es Cricket Club
    N/CH/CXG WD3...............14 B3

Cherry Tree JMI School
    WATN WD24..................10 B5
Chorleywood Golf Club
    RKW/CH/CXG WD3............24 C1
Chorleywood Health Centre
    RKW/CH/CXG WD3............24 B1
Chorleywood Primary
    RKW/CH/CXG WD3............24 B3
Christ Church CE
    Primary School
    RKW/CH/CXG WD3............25 E1
Coates Way JMI School
    ....11 F2
Colnbrook School
    OXHEY WD19.................34 D1
Colne Bridge Retail Park
    WAT WD17....................3 K7
Colne Valley Retail Park
    WAT WD17....................3 K6
Colonial Business Park
    WATN WD24..................18 D3
Community Mental Health
    Centre
    GSTN WD25..................10 D3
Corus Hotel
    BORE WD6...................32 B4
County Council Offices
    BUSH WD23..................30 C4
Cowley Hill Primary School
    BORE WD6...................23 E3
CP House Business Centre
    BUSH WD23..................19 G3
Delrow School
    GSTN WD25..................20 B3
Divine Saviour RC
    Primary School
    ABLGY WD5....................9 G1
Eastbury Farm JMI School
    NTHWD HA6..................34 A3
Edge Grove School
    GSTN WD25..................20 B1
Elstree Aerodrome
    BORE WD6...................21 E5
Elstree Golf & Country Club
    BORE WD6...................22 A5
Elstree Studios
    BORE WD6...................22 D5
Elstree Way Clinic
    BORE WD6...................23 E4
Fairbrook Medical Centre
    BORE WD6...................23 E4
Fair Field Junior School
    RAD WD7....................12 D5
Falconer Special School
    BUSH WD23..................29 G2
Field Infant School
    WATW WD18...................3 C6
Field Junior School
    WATW WD18...................3 H6
Fisher Industrial Estate
    WATW WD18...................3 G7
Francis Combe School
    GSTN WD25..................10 D1
Frithwood Primary School
    NTHWD HA6..................34 A5
Furzehill School
    BORE WD6...................32 D1
Garston Clinic
    GSTN WD25..................10 C5
Garston JMI School
    GSTN WD25..................11 E4
Garston Manor Special School
    GSTN WD25..................10 D1
Garston Medical Centre
    GSTN WD25..................10 D5

Gazelda Industrial Estate
    WAT WD17....................3 J6
Greatham Road
    Industrial Estate
    BUSH WD23..................29 F1
Green End Business Centre
    RKW/CH/CXG WD3............15 F1
Greenfield Primary School
    OXHEY WD19.................34 D4
Grimsdyke First & Middle
    School
    PIN HA5....................35 G5
Grims Dyke Golf Club
    PIN HA5....................35 H4
The Grove Hotel
    RKW/CH/CXG WD3............17 F1
The Haberdashers Askes
    School for Boys
    BORE WD6...................21 G5
Haberdashers RUFC
    BORE WD6...................22 C2
Happy Valley
    Industrial Estate
    KGLGY WD4....................5 E2
Harkness Industrial Estate
    BORE WD6...................32 D1
The Harlequin Shopping
    Centre
    WAT WD17....................3 H1
Hartspring Industrial Park
    BUSH WD23..................19 H4
Hartspring Sports Centre
    BUSH WD23..................19 H4
Harvey Road Primary School
    RKW/CH/CXG WD3............26 D3
Hertsmere Jewish
    Primary School
    RAD WD7....................21 H2
Hertswood School &
    Sports Centre
    BORE WD6...................23 F3
Highwood Primary School
    BUSH WD23..................19 F3
Hille Business Centre
    WATN WD24..................18 C3
Hill Farm Industrial Estate
    GSTN WD25..................10 A2
Holiday Inn
    BORE WD6...................23 H5
Holly Industrial Park
    WATN WD24..................18 D3
Holmshill School
    BORE WD6...................23 F4
Holy Rood RC Infant School
    WAT WD17....................9 G5
Holy Rood RC Junior School
    WAT WD17....................9 G5
Holywell School
    WATN WD24..................28 A3
Home Park Industrial Estate
    KGLGY WD4....................5 E5
Immanuel College
    BUSH WD23..................30 D4
Innkeepers Lodge
    BORE WD6...................23 F4
International University
    BUSH WD23..................29 G1
Kenilworth Primary School
    BORE WD6...................23 G5
Kinetic Business Centre
    BORE WD6...................22 C5
Kings Langley Primary School
    KGLGY WD4....................4 C2
Kings Park Industrial Estate
    KGLGY WD4....................5 E3

Kingsway Junior School
    GSTN WD25..................10 B3
Knutsford School
    WATN WD24..................19 E2
Laharna Trading Estate
    WATN WD24..................18 D2
Laings Sports Ground
    BAR EN5....................33 H1
Laurance Haines School
    WATW WD18..................28 B3
Lea Farm Junior School
    GSTN WD25..................11 E3
Leavesden Green JMI School
    GSTN WD25..................10 B3
Leavesden Hospital
    ABLGY WD5....................6 B5
Lismarrine Industrial Park
    BORE WD6...................31 G3
Little Green Junior School
    RKW/CH/CXG WD3............16 D5
Little Reddings
    Primary School
    BUSH WD23..................30 A2
Lodge Sun Sports Club
    WAT WD17...................17 H3
Long Island Hotel
    RKW/CH/CXG WD3............26 A4
Lyndhurst Middle School
    BORE WD6...................22 C3
Malvern Way Infant School
    RKW/CH/CXG WD3............27 F2
Manor Place Industrial Estate
    BORE WD6...................23 F5
Meadow Wood School
    BUSH WD23..................30 B2
The Medical Centre
    WAT WD17....................2 E1
Merchant Taylors School
    NTHWD HA6..................27 H5
Merry Hill Infant School
    BUSH WD23..................30 A4
Meryfield Primary School
    BORE WD6...................22 C3
Metropolis Centre
    BORE WD6...................22 D5
Metropolitan Police
    Bushey Sports Ground
    BUSH WD23..................19 H5
Monksmead School
    BORE WD6...................23 F5
Moor Park Industrial Estate
    WATW WD18..................27 F4
Mount Pleasant Lane
    J & I School
    LCOL/BKTW AL2...............7 H2
Mowat Industrial Estate
    WATN WD24..................18 D2
Nascot Wood Infant School
    WAT WD17...................18 B2
North Watford Cemetery
    GSTN WD25..................10 B4
North Watford Health Clinic
    GSTN WD25..................10 D3
Oaklands College
    BORE WD6...................23 F4
Odhams Industrial Estate
    WATN WD24..................18 D1
Odhams Trading Estate
    WATN WD24..................10 B5
    WATN WD24..................10 D5
Old Merchant Taylors
    Sports Club
    RKW/CH/CXG WD3............27 E1
Orchard Primary School
    WATN WD24..................10 A5

Oxhey Infant School
OXHEY WD19 ....**29** F3

Oxhey Park Golf Centre
OXHEY WD19 ....**29** E5

Oxhey Wood Primary School
OXHEY WD19 ....**34** D3

Palace Theatre
WAT WD17 ....**3** F3

Paramount Industrial Estate
WATN WD24 ....**18** D2

Park Avenue Clinic
WAT WD17 ....**2** D1

Parkside Primary School
BORE WD6 ....**22** C2

Parmiters School
GSTN WD25 ....**6** D5

Peerglow Industrial Estate
WATW WD18 ....**27** E4

Pinner Hill Golf Club
PIN HA5 ....**34** C5

Porters Park Golf Club
RAD WD7 ....**13** H3

Premier Inn
BORE WD6 ....**23** G5
GSTN WD25 ....**11** E3
KGLGY WD4 ....**4** C2
WAT WD17 ....**3** J4
WATW WD18 ....**27** H2

Pump House Theatre
WAT WD17 ....**3** J6

Queens School
BUSH WD23 ....**19** G5

Radlett Cricket Club
RAD WD7 ....**21** G1

Radlett Lodge School
RAD WD7 ....**13** H1

Radlett Preparatory School
RAD WD7 ....**21** H2

Ramada Hotel
GSTN WD25 ....**20** B5

Rickmansworth School
RKW/CH/CXG WD3 ....**26** C3

Rickmansworth Sports Club
RKW/CH/CXG WD3 ....**26** B3

Rosary Priory High School
BUSH WD23 ....**30** D3

Royal Masonic School for Girls
RKW/CH/CXG WD3 ....**26** A3

Royal National Orthopaedic Hospital
STAN HA7 ....**31** G5

Rudolf Steiner School
KGLGY WD4 ....**4** B3

The Russell School
RKW/CH/CXG WD3 ....**24** A1

Sacred Heart RC Primary School
OXHEY WD19 ....**29** G3

Saffron Green Primary School
BORE WD6 ....**33** H1

St Anthonys RC Primary School
WATW WD18 ....**27** H2

St Catherine of Sienna RC Primary School
GSTN WD25 ....**11** E1

St Clement Danes School
RKW/CH/CXG WD3 ....**14** C4

St Hildas School
BUSH WD23 ....**30** A4

St Joan of Arc RC School
RKW/CH/CXG WD3 ....**26** B4

St Johns Infant School
RAD WD7 ....**13** E4

St Johns RC Primary School
RKW/CH/CXG WD3 ....**25** G5

St Johns School
NTHWD HA6 ....**34** C5

St Josephs RC Primary School
OXHEY WD19 ....**34** C2

St Margarets School
BUSH WD23 ....**29** H4

St Meryl JMI School
OXHEY WD19 ....**35** F2

St Michaels RC School
GSTN WD25 ....**10** D1

St Nicholas School
BORE WD6 ....**32** B3

St Pauls CE Primary School
KGLGY WD4 ....**9** E3

St Peters JMI School
RKW/CH/CXG WD3 ....**25** G5

St Teresa's RC Primary School
BORE WD6 ....**23** E4

Sandown Road Industrial Estate
WATN WD24 ....**18** D1

Shakespeare Industrial Estate
WATN WD24 ....**18** B2

Sheepcot Medical Centre
GSTN WD25 ....**10** D3

Shepherd Primary School
RKW/CH/CXG WD3 ....**25** F5

Sir James Altham Swimming Pool
OXHEY WD19 ....**35** F4

Skidmore Clinic
RKW/CH/CXG WD3 ....**26** B5

Stanborough Primary School
GSTN WD25 ....**10** D4

Stanborough School
GSTN WD25 ....**10** C4

Stirling Industrial Centre
BORE WD6 ....**33** G2

Stirling Retail Park
BORE WD6 ....**33** G3

Summerswood Primary School
BORE WD6 ....**33** E1

Sunderland Estate
KGLGY WD4 ....**5** E3

Tabard RFC
RAD WD7 ....**21** G1

Tanners Wood Primary School
ABLGY WD5 ....**9** H1

Thistle Hotel
LCOL/BKTW AL2 ....**7** G1

Vale Industrial Estate
WATW WD18 ....**27** F5

Vicarage Road Cemetery
WATW WD18 ....**2** D5

Vue Cinema
GSTN WD25 ....**10** D2

Warren Dell Primary School
OXHEY WD19 ....**34** D2

Watersmeet Centre
RKW/CH/CXG WD3 ....**26** B4

Waterways Heritage Museum
RKW/CH/CXG WD3 ....**26** B5

Watford Arches Retail Park
WAT WD17 ....**3** J7

Watford Business Centre
WAT WD17 ....**2** E2

Watford County Court
WAT WD17 ....**18** C4

Watford FC & Saracens RFC (Vicarage Road Stadium)
WATW WD18 ....**2** E6

Watford General Hospital
WATW WD18 ....**2** E7

Watford Grammar School for Boys
WATW WD18 ....

Watford Grammar School for Girls
WATW WD18 ....

Watford Museum
WATW WD18 ....

Watford Sports & Leisure Centre
GSTN WD25 ....

The Wenta Business Centre
WATN WD24 ....

Westfield Community Technology College
WATW WD18 ....

West Herts Business Centre
BORE WD6 ....

West Herts College (Cassio Campus)
WAT WD17 ....

West Herts College (Leggatts Campus)
WATN WD24 ....

West Herts College (Watford Campus)
WAT WD17 ....

West Herts Crematorium
GSTN WD25 ....

West Herts Golf Club
RKW/CH/CXG WD3 ....

William Penn Leisure Centre
RKW/CH/CXG WD3 ....

Wolsey Business Park
WATW WD18 ....

Woodhall School
OXHEY WD19 ....

Woodlands Primary School
BORE WD6 ....

Woodside Stadium
GSTN WD25 ....

Yavneh College
BORE WD6 ....

York House School
RKW/CH/CXG WD3 ....

Acknowledgements

Schools address data provided by Education Direct.

Petrol station information supplied by Johnsons.

Garden centre information provided by:

Garden Centre Association  Britains best garden centres

Wyevale Garden Centres

The statement on the front cover of this atlas is sourced, selected and quoted from a reader comment and feedback form received in 2004